I0427315

I am grateful to God for everything! And I believe that the meaning of life is to give meaning to other lives. A.M., you are the meaning of my life.
Lov U

Vinicius Borges
2024

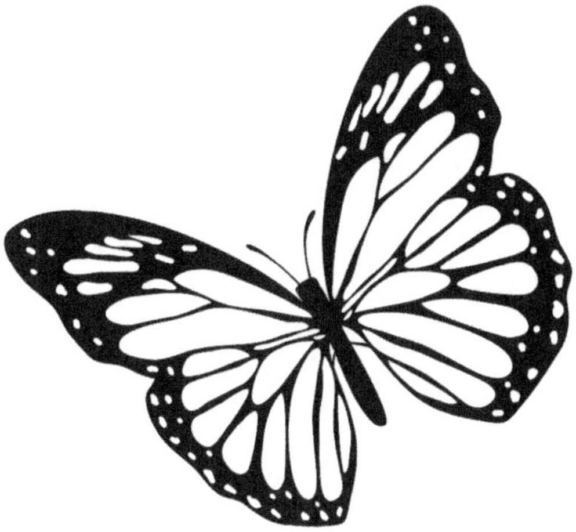

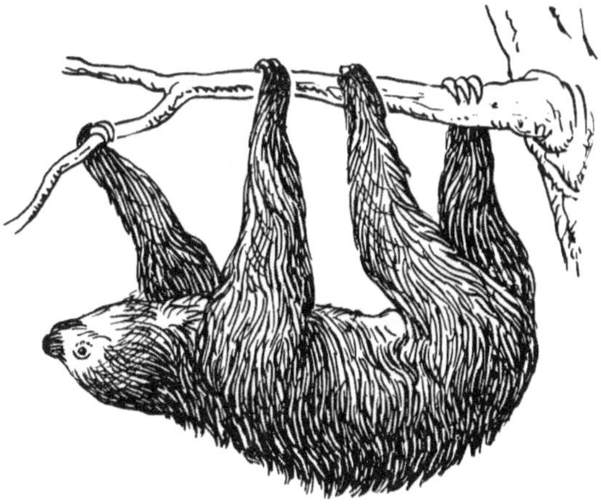

This Book Belongs to:

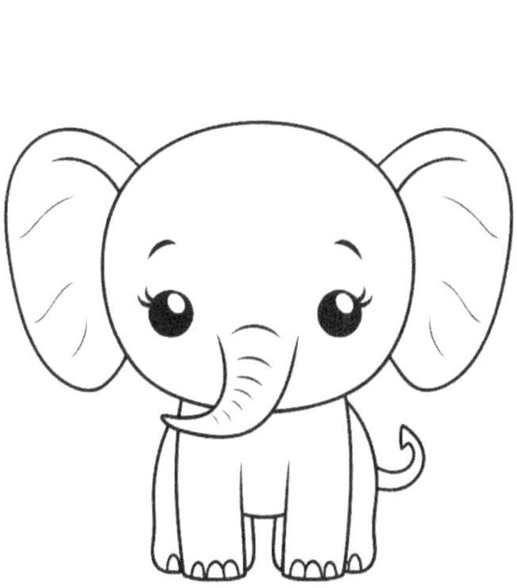

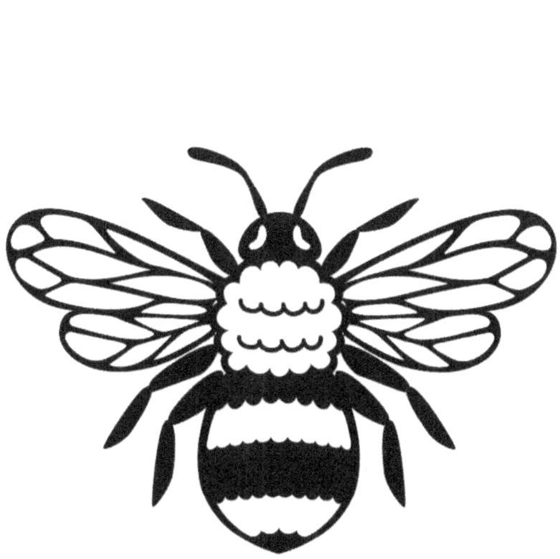

Test Color Page

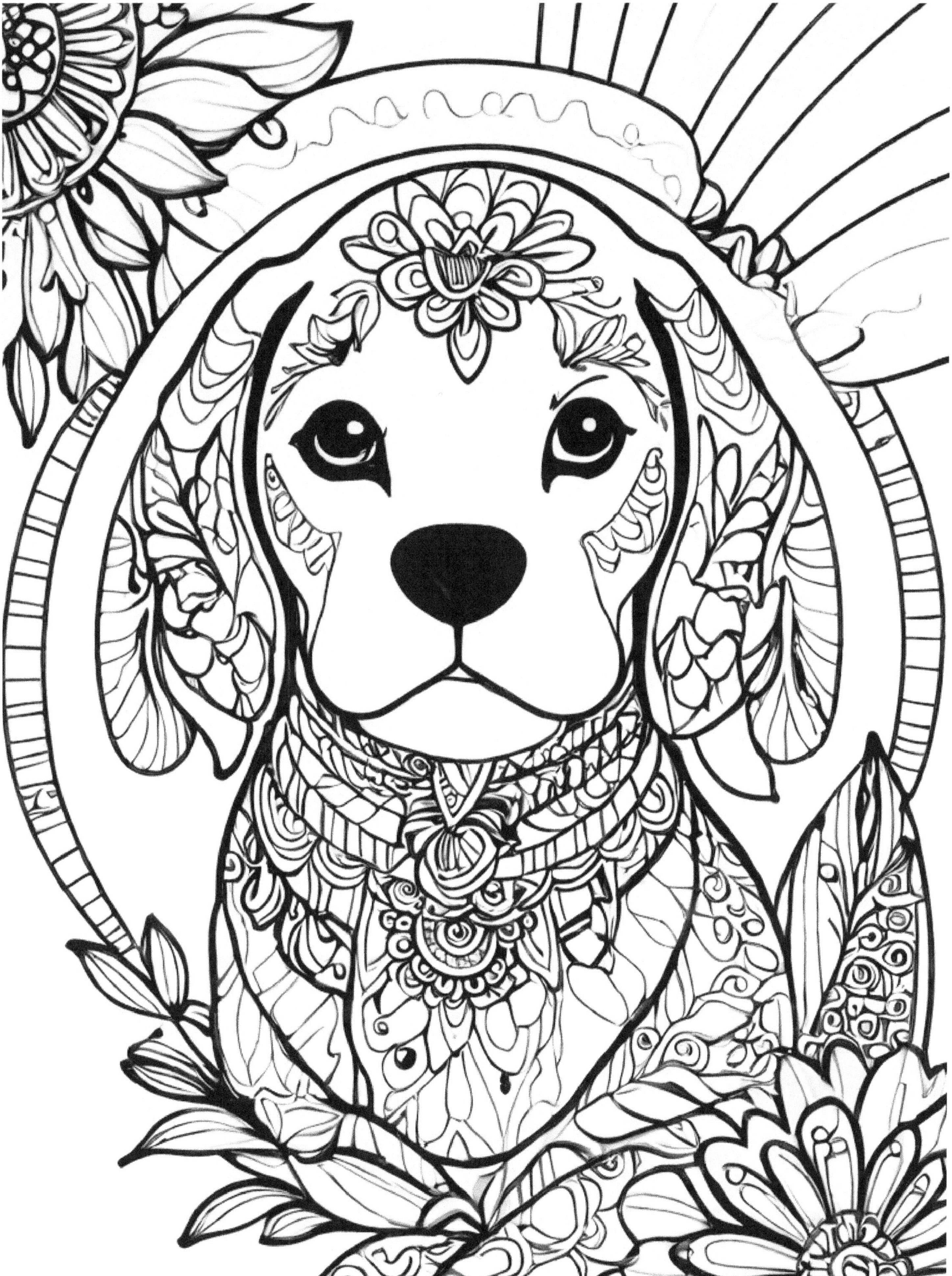

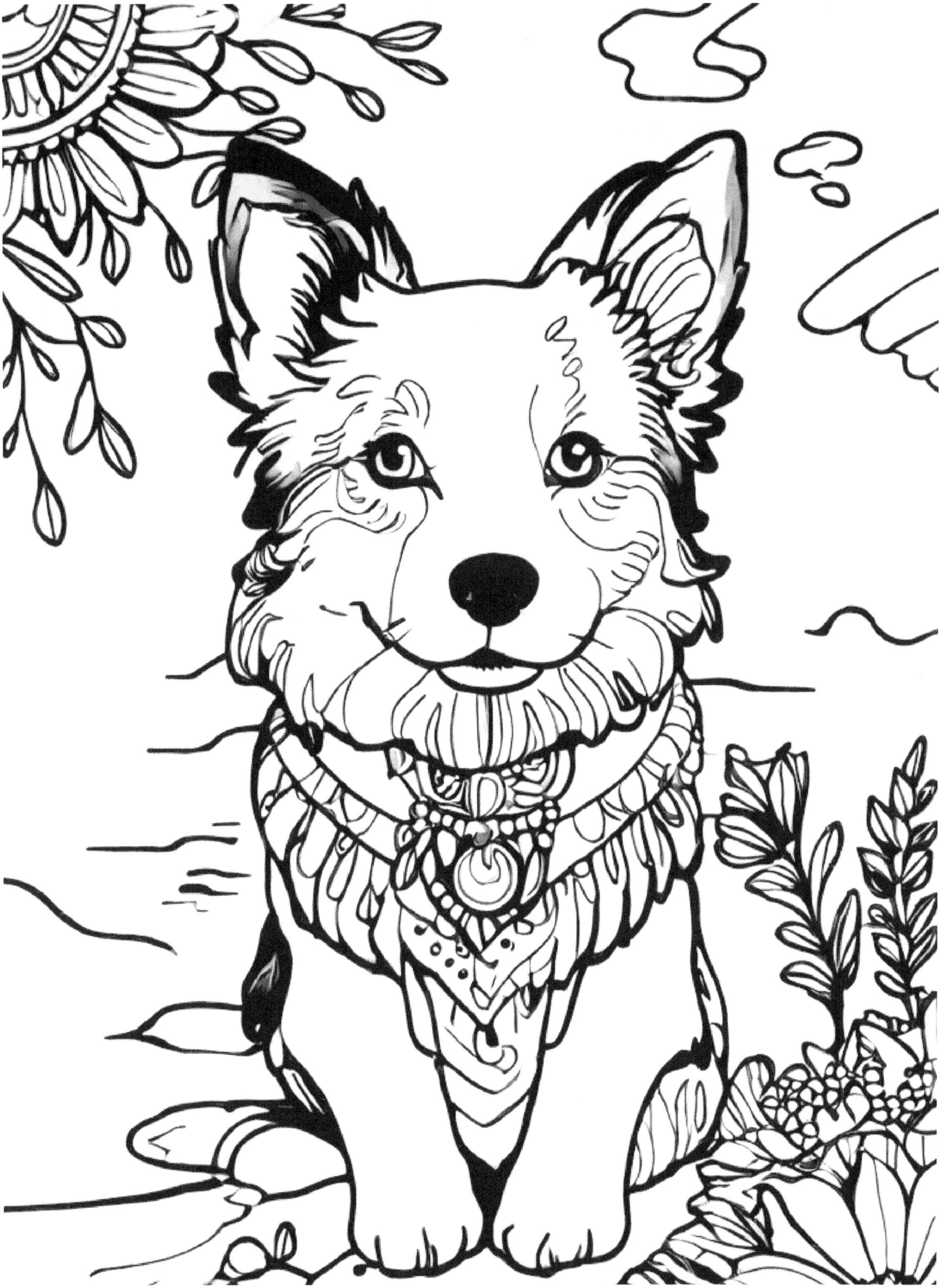

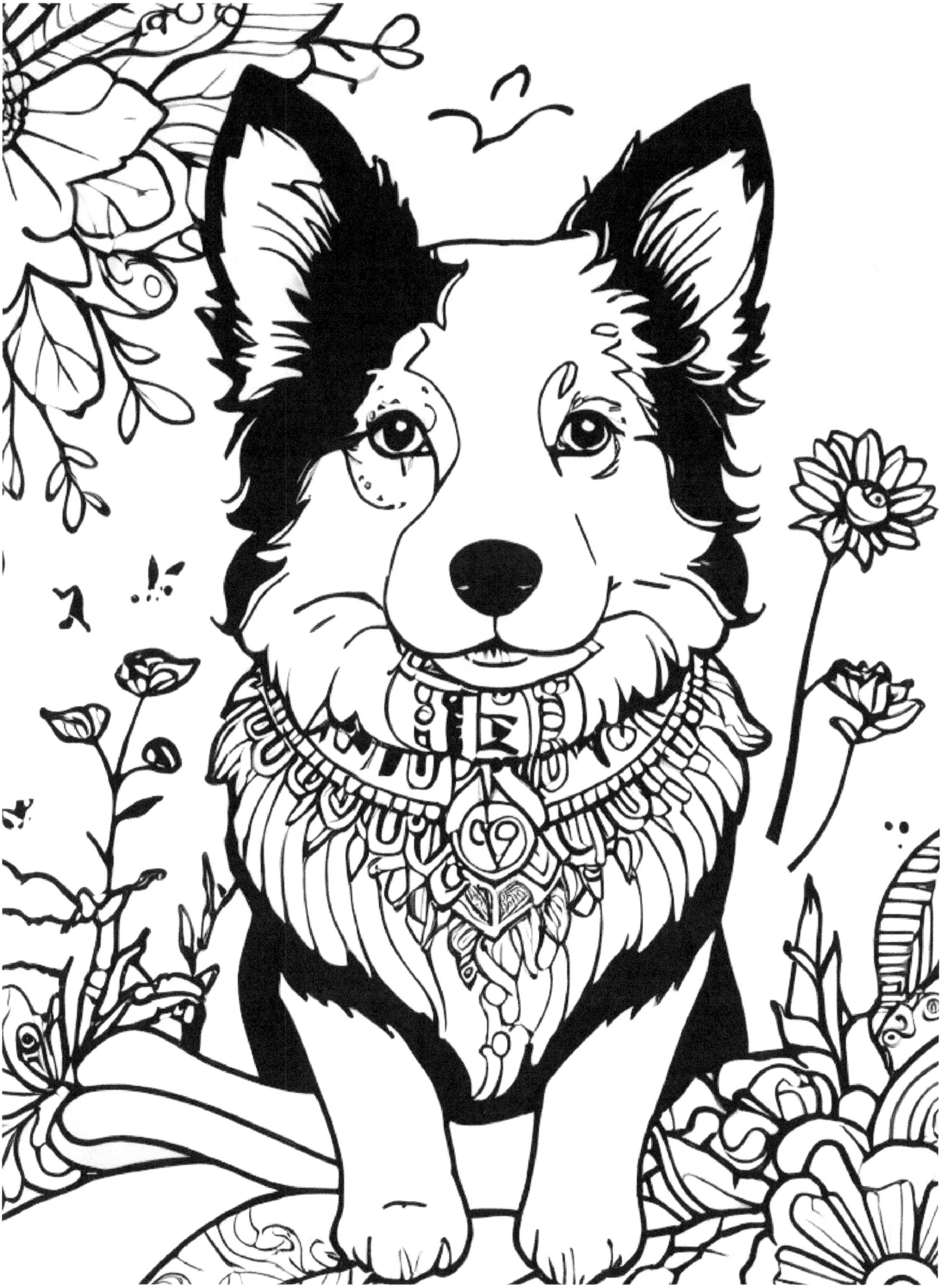

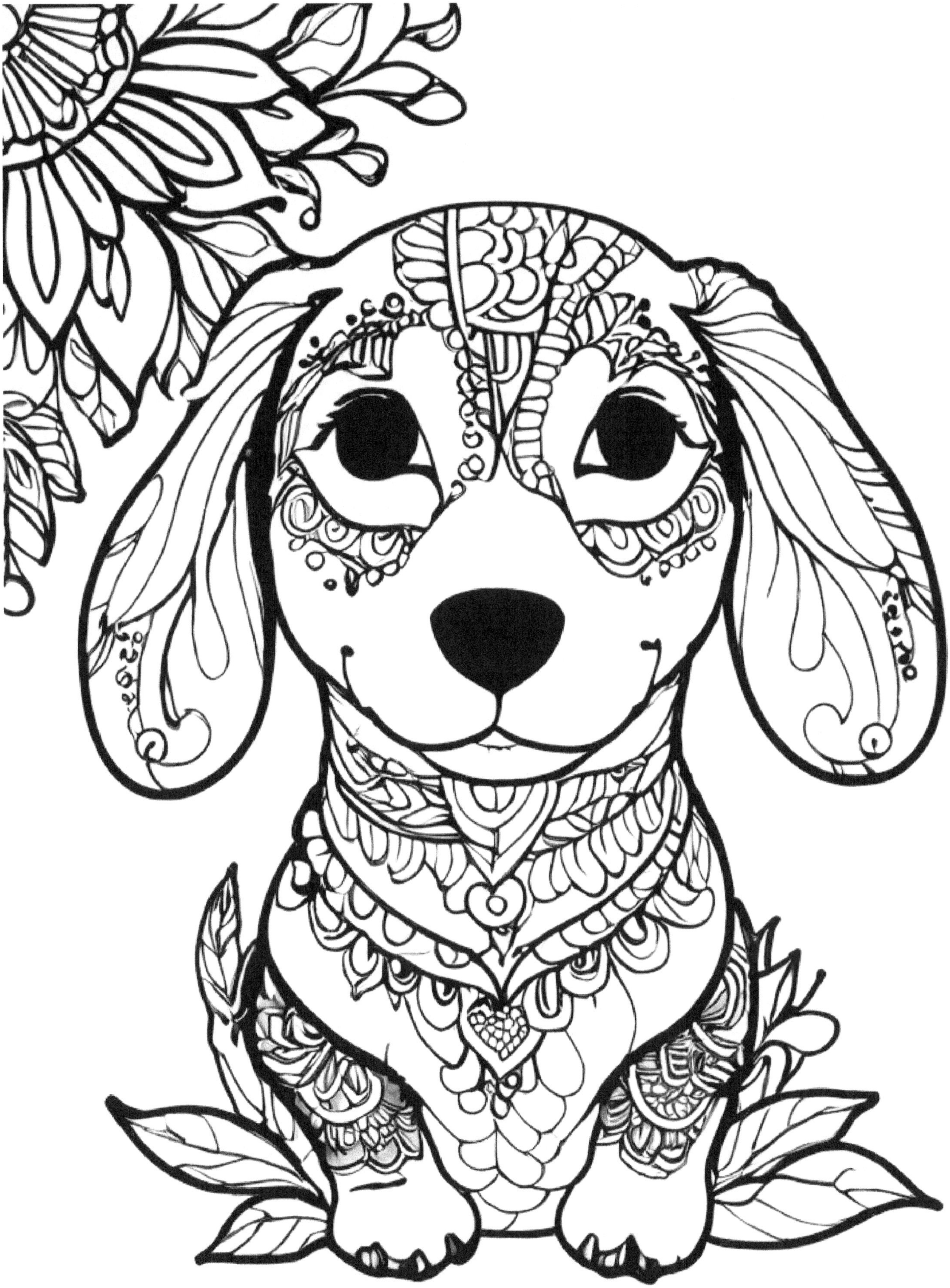

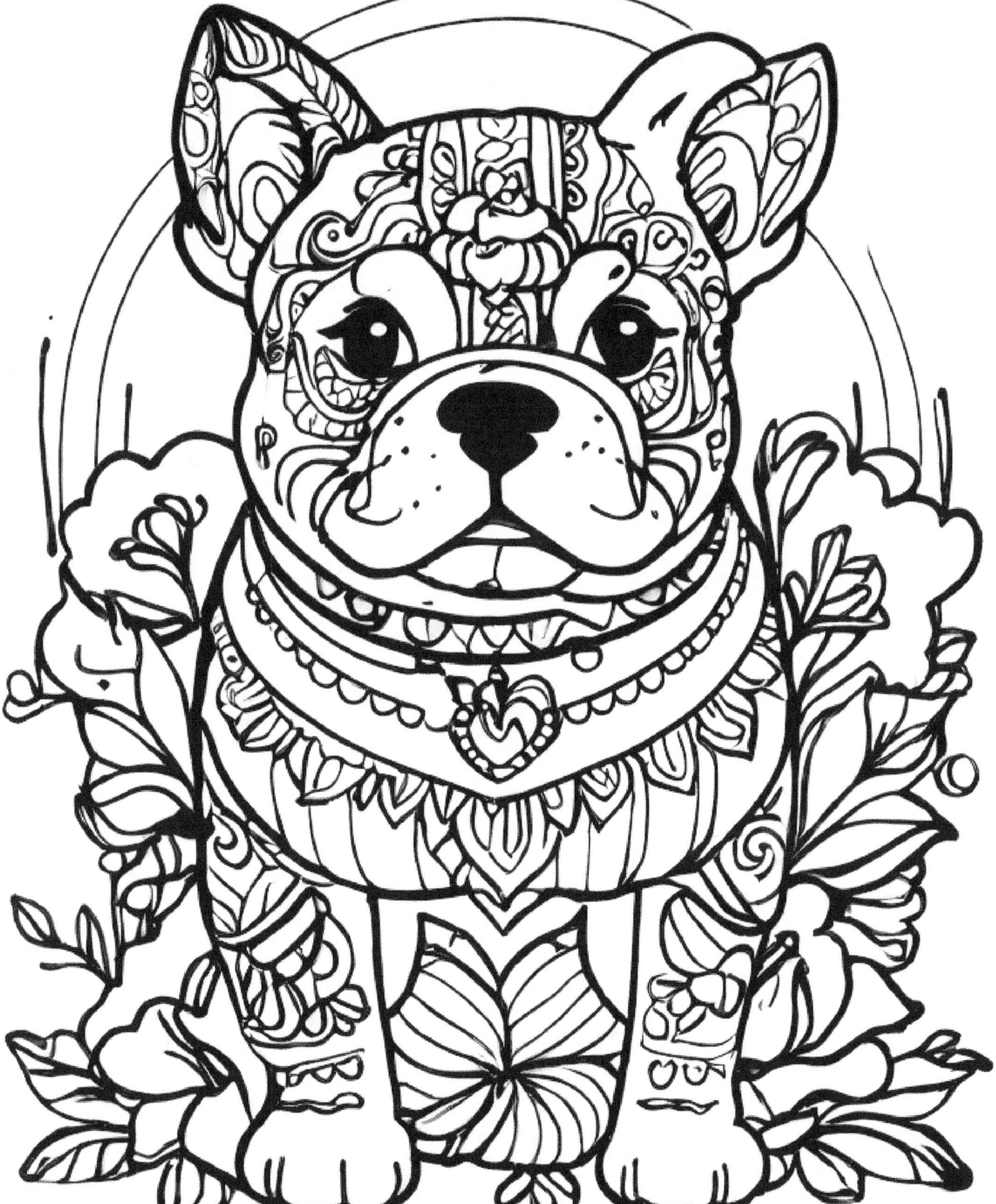

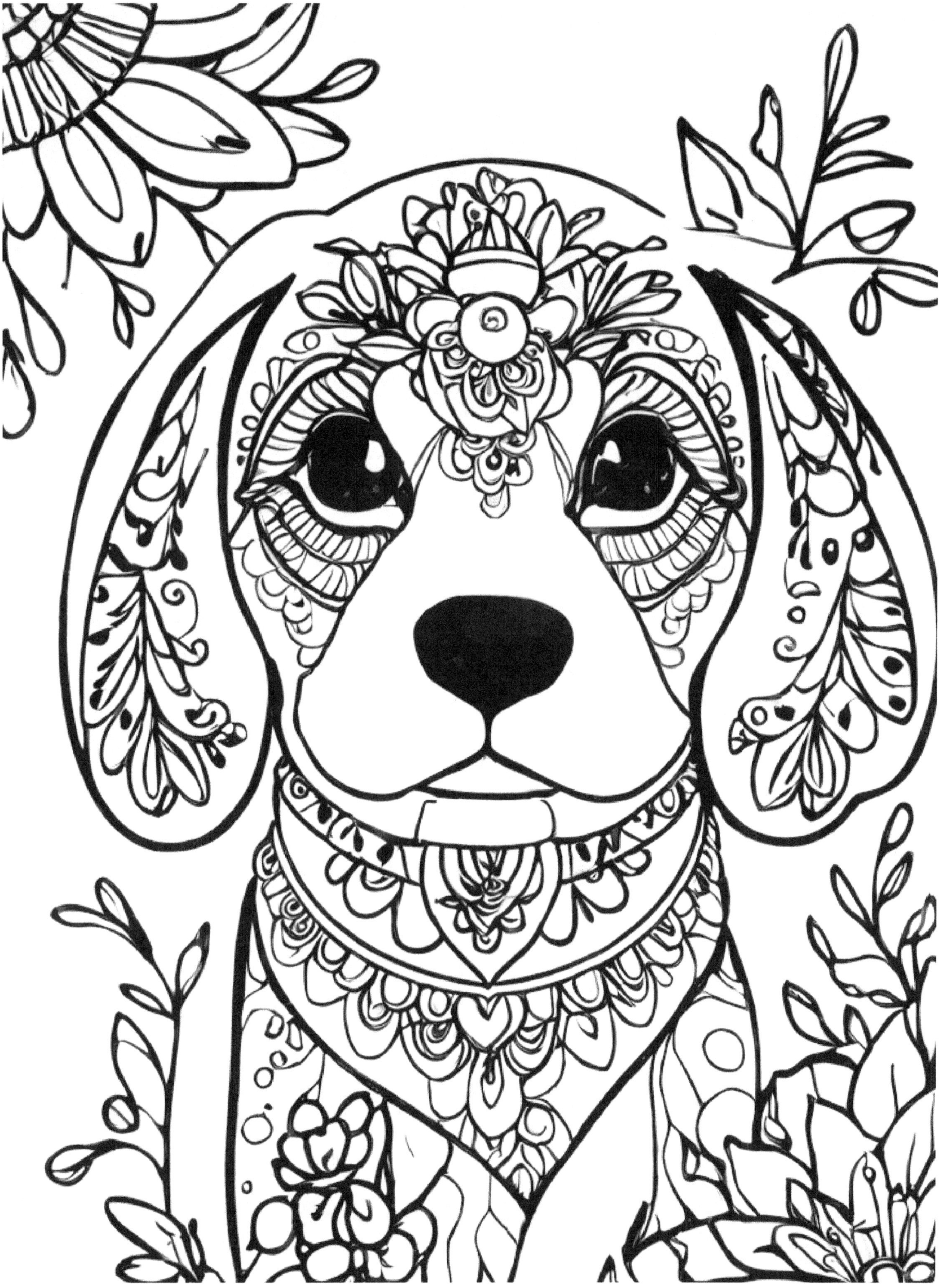

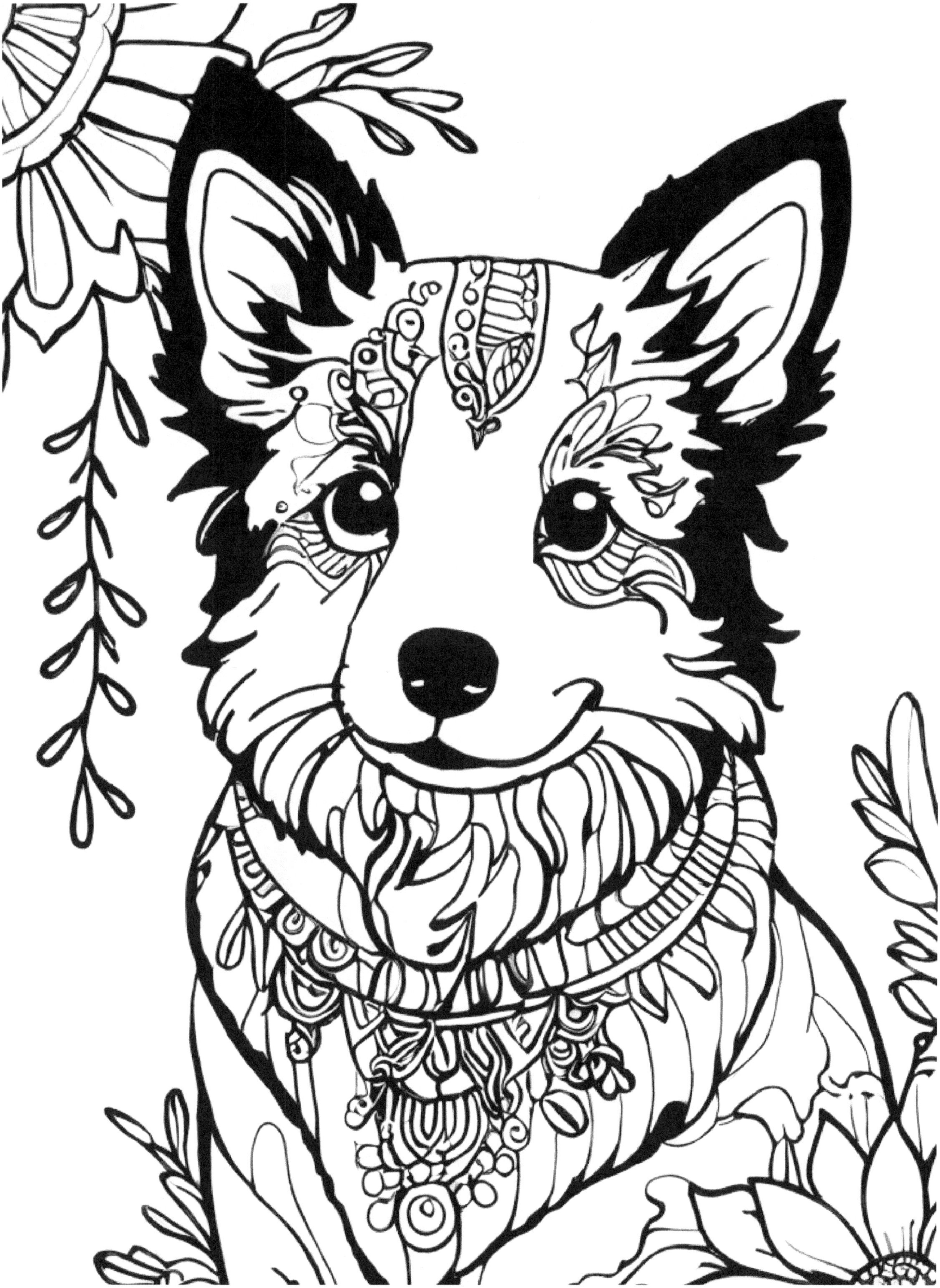

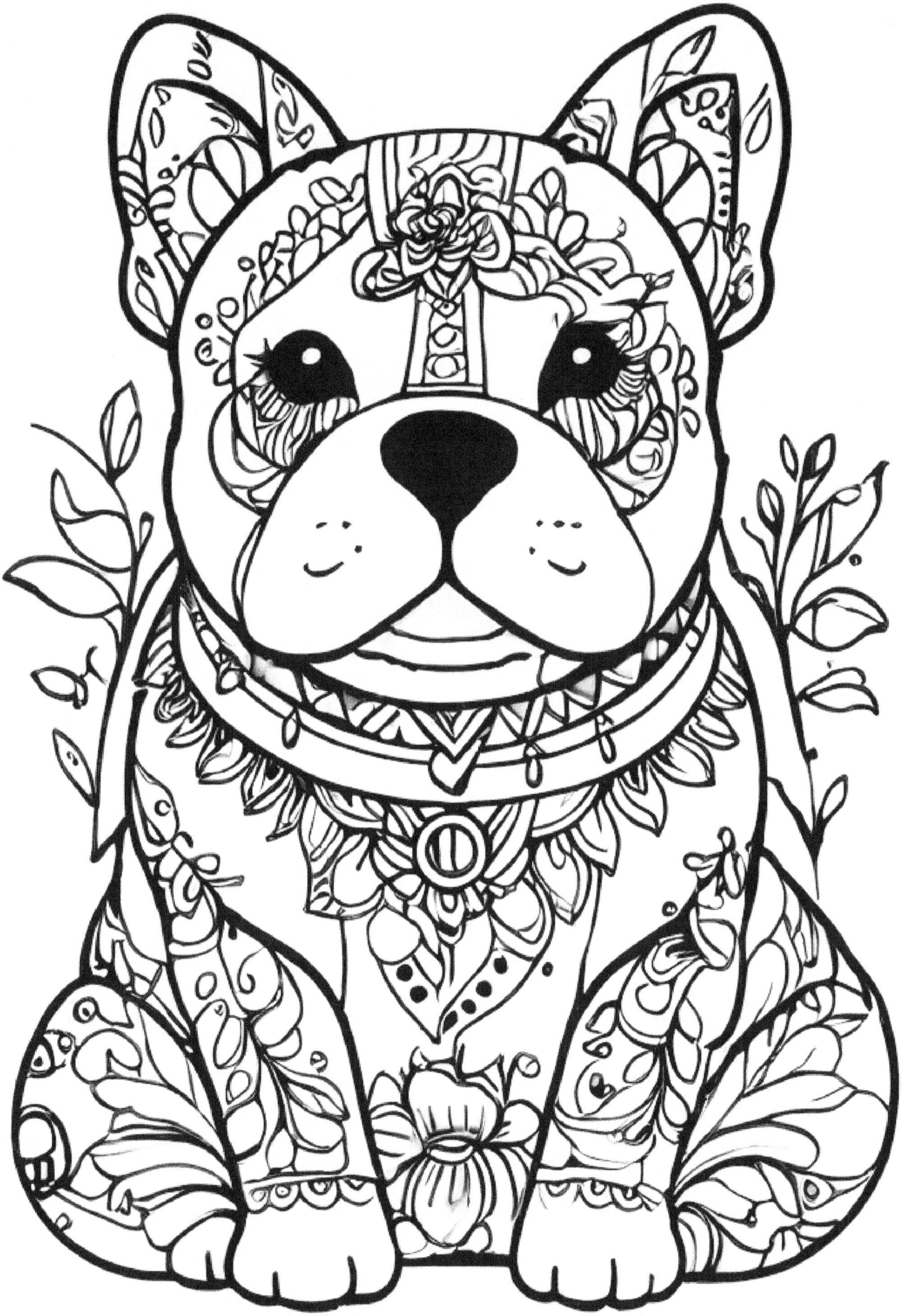

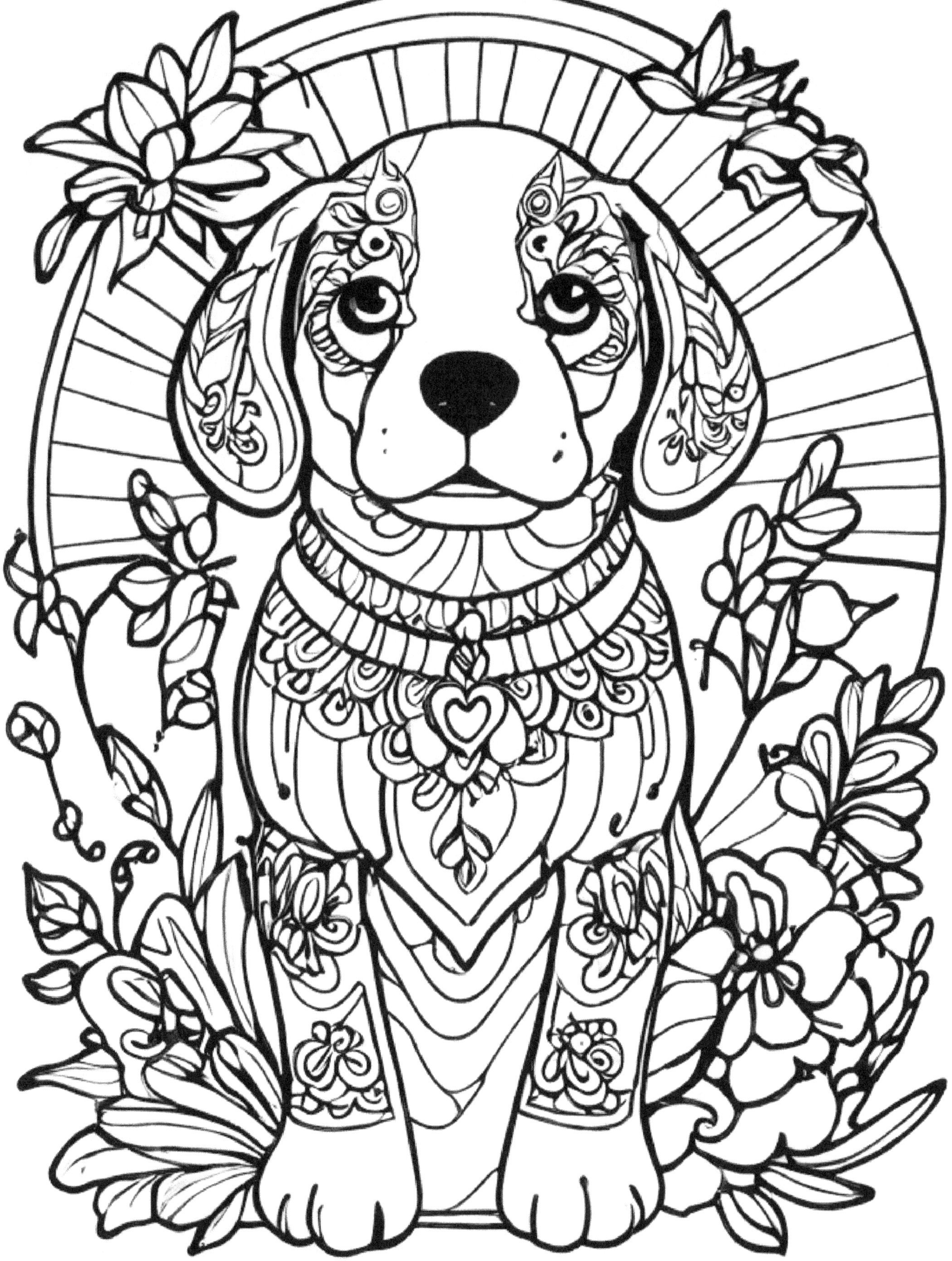

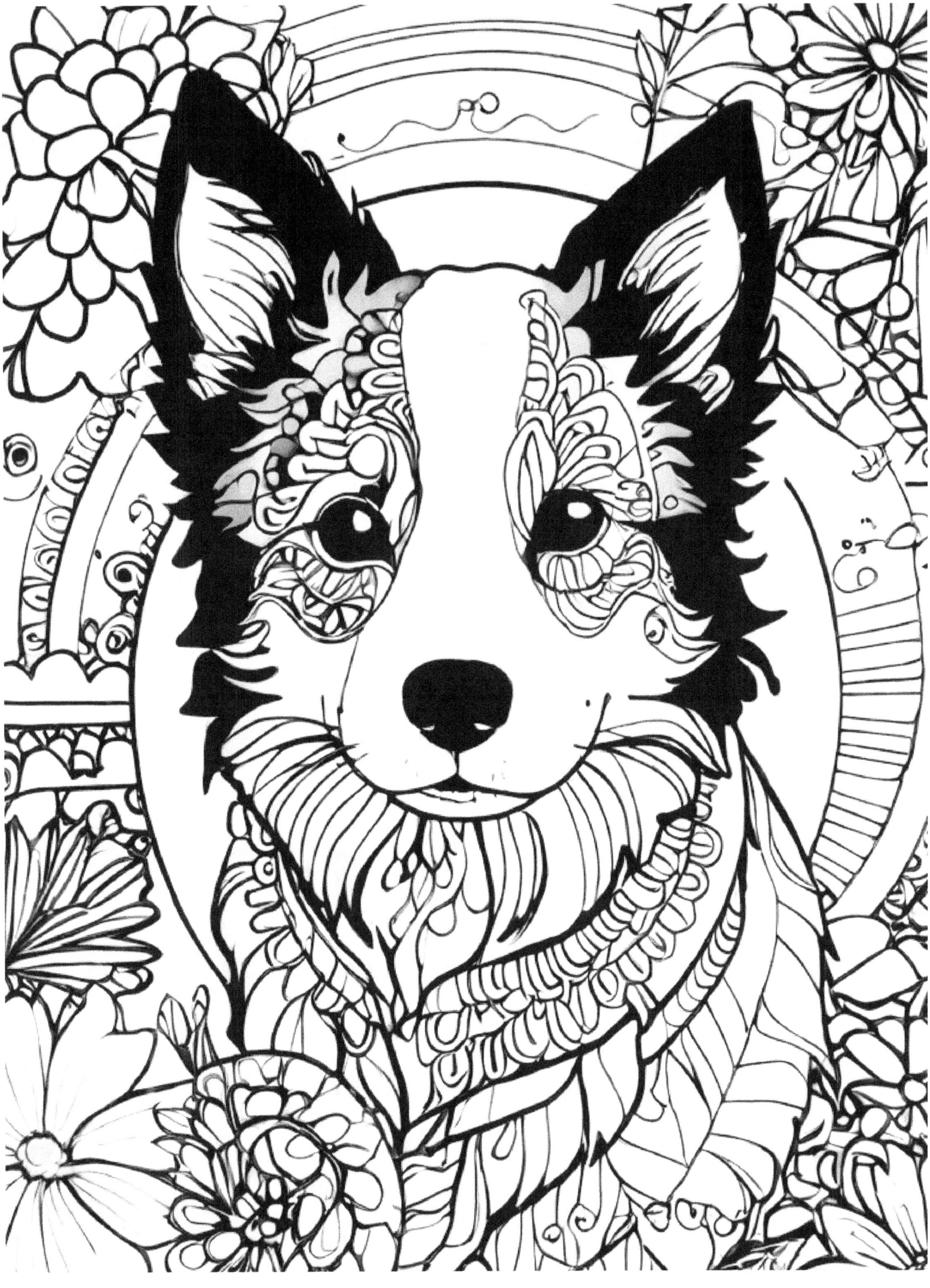

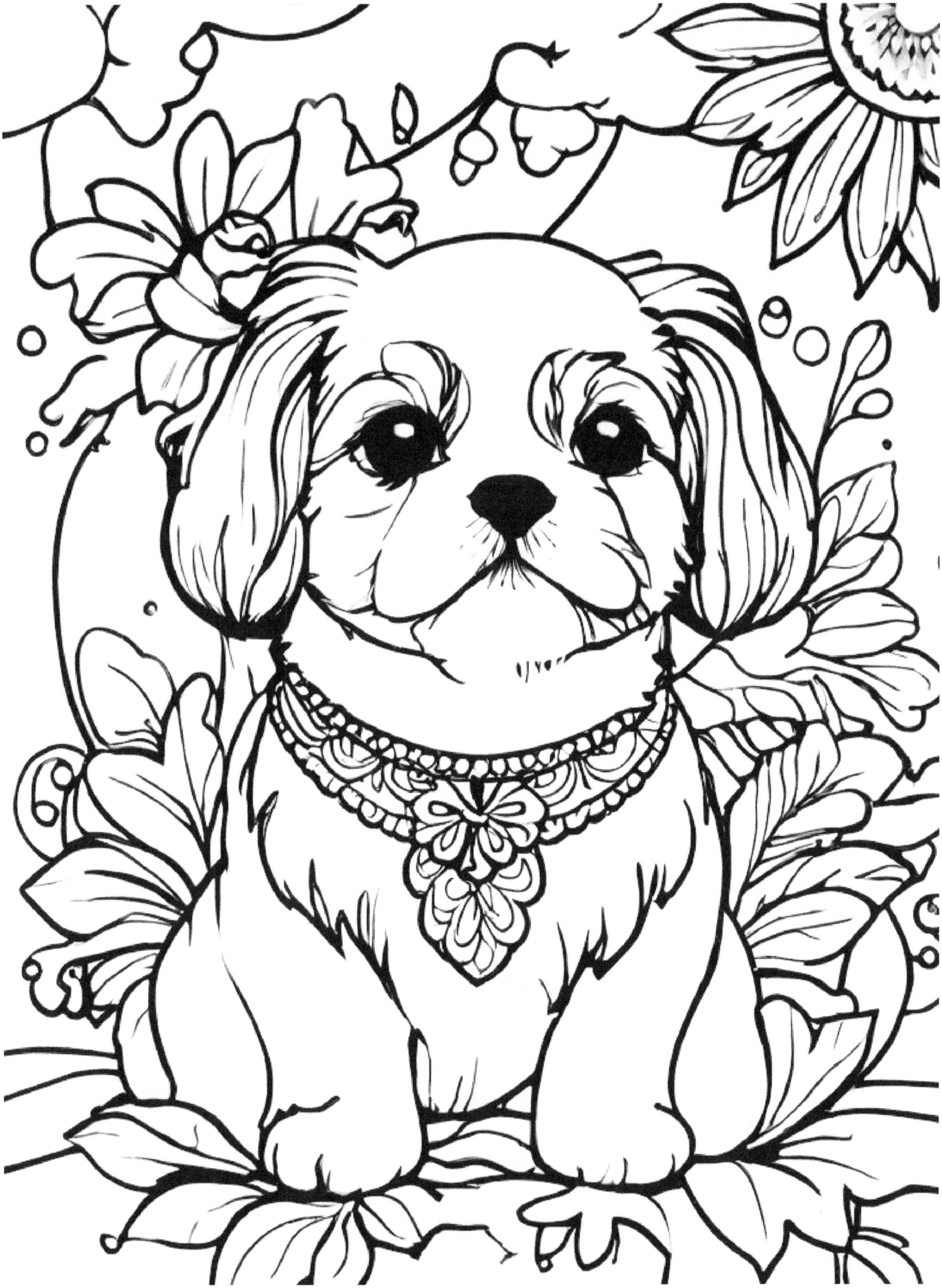

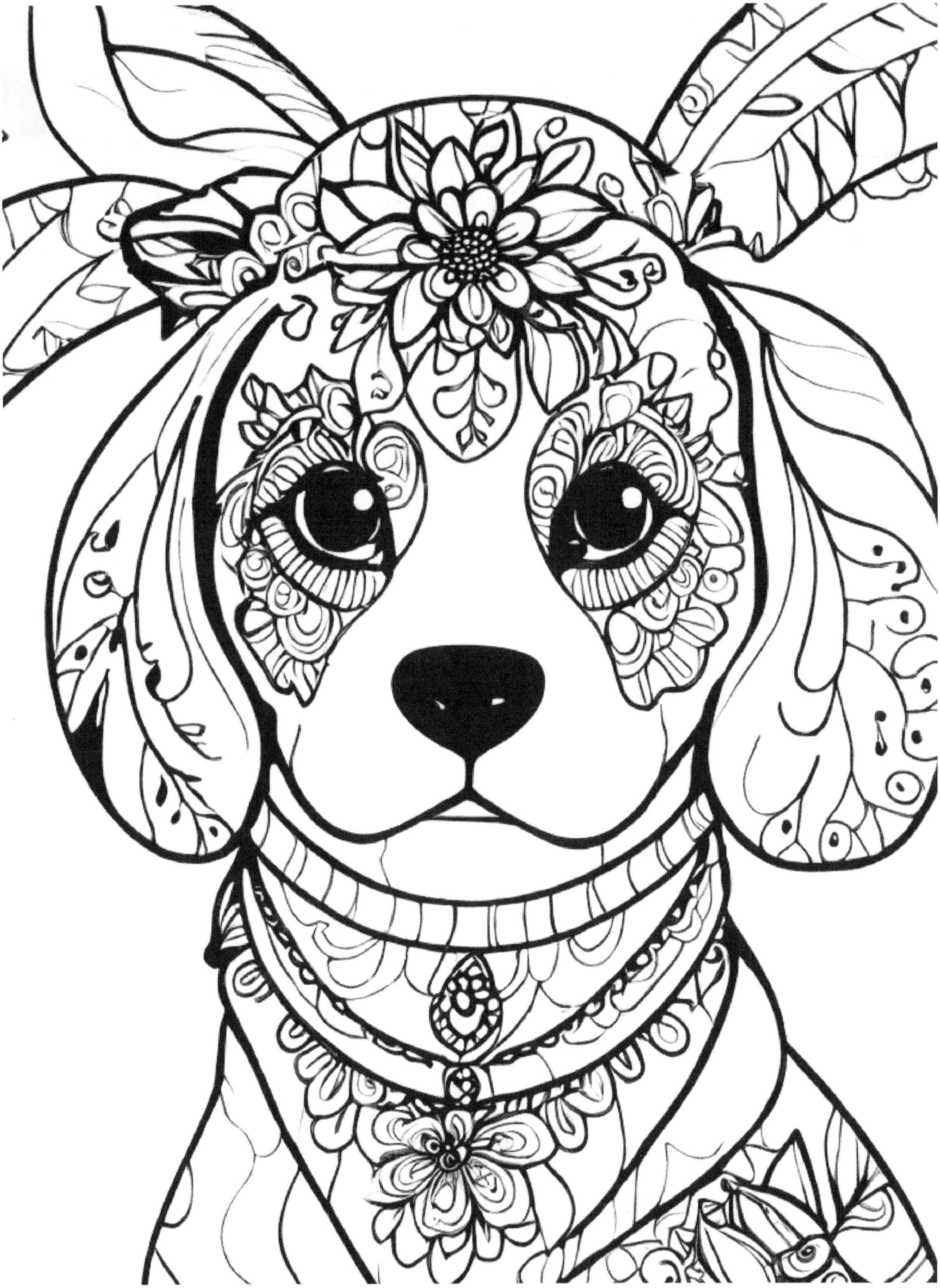

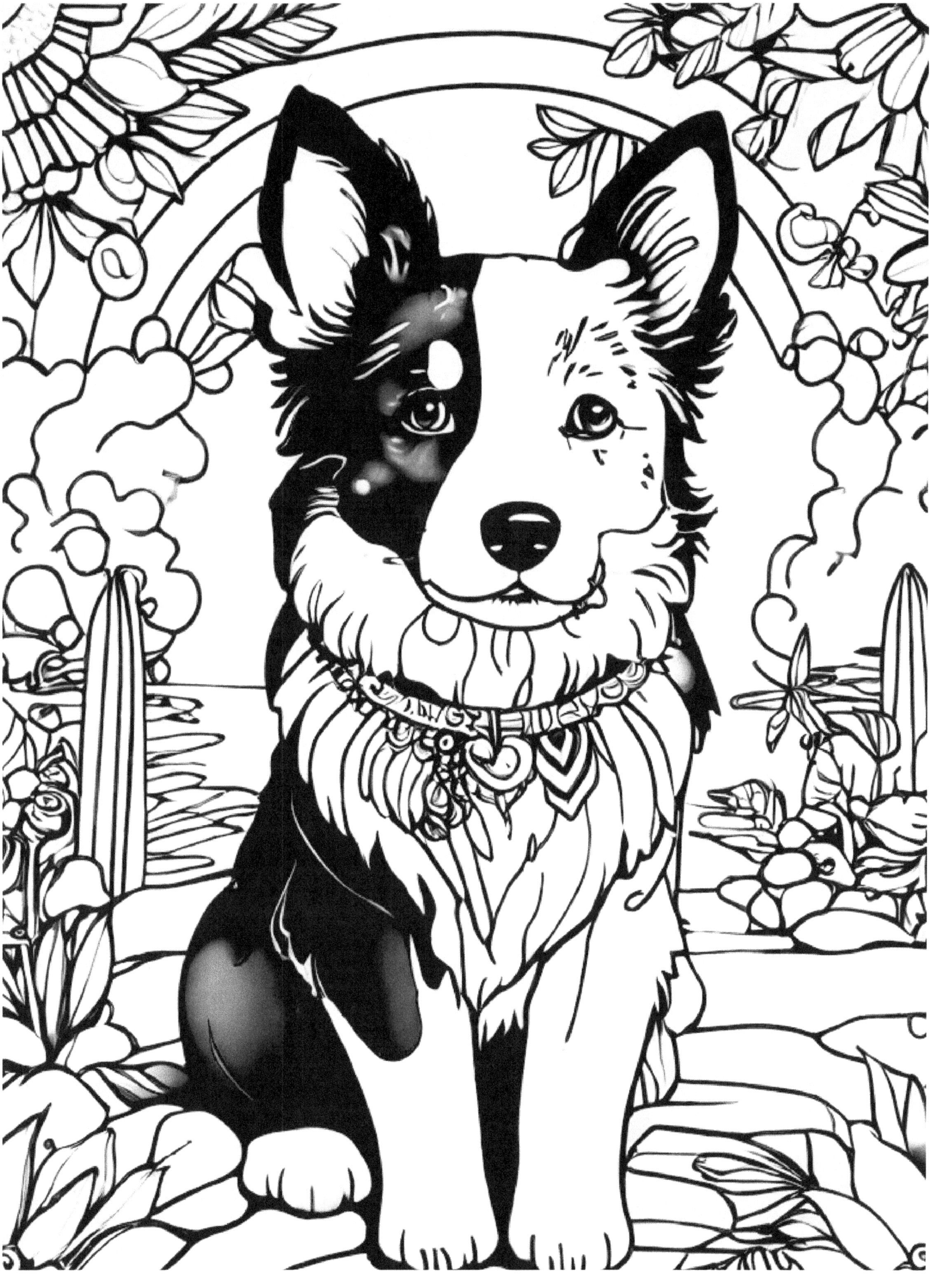

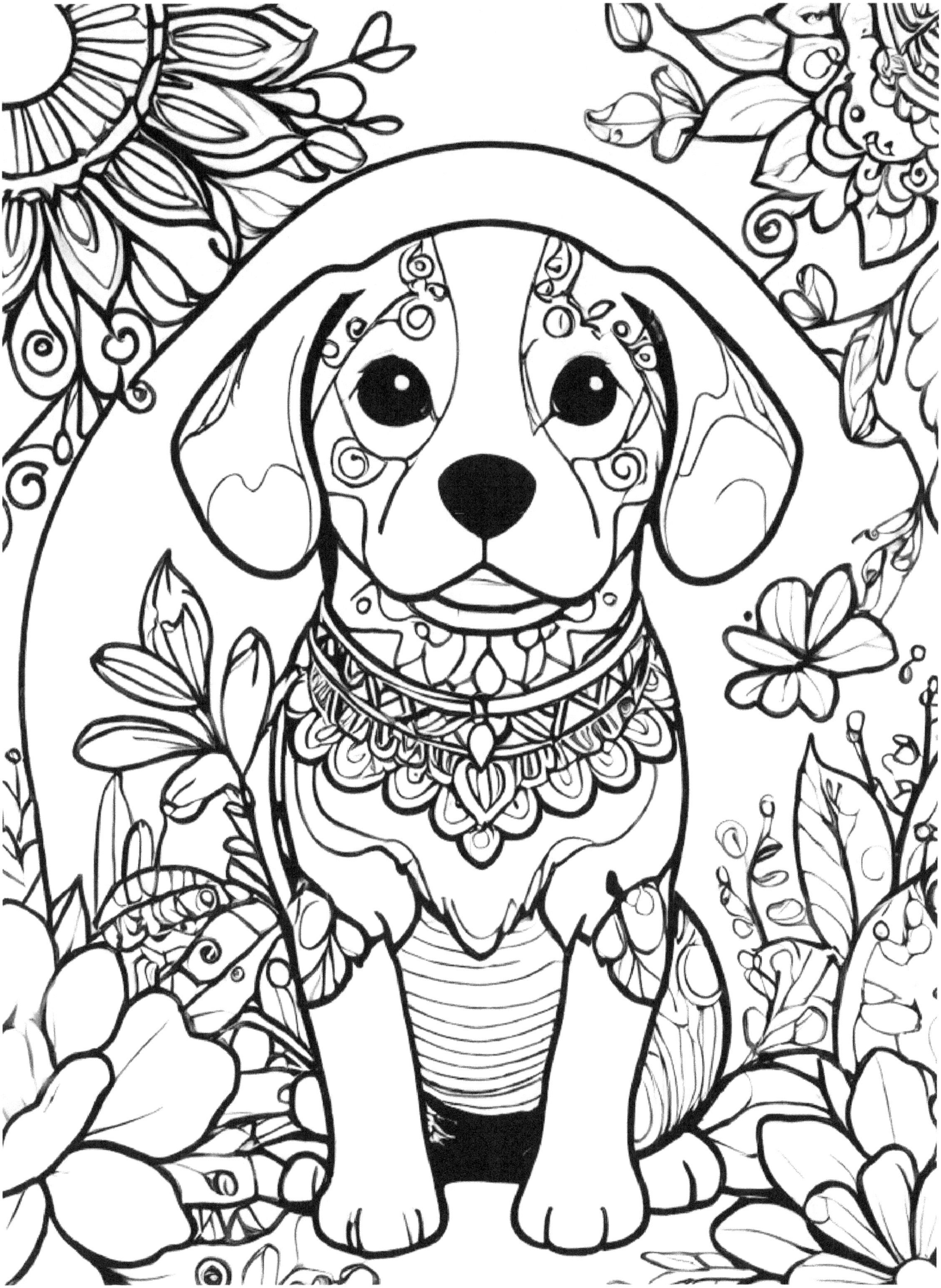

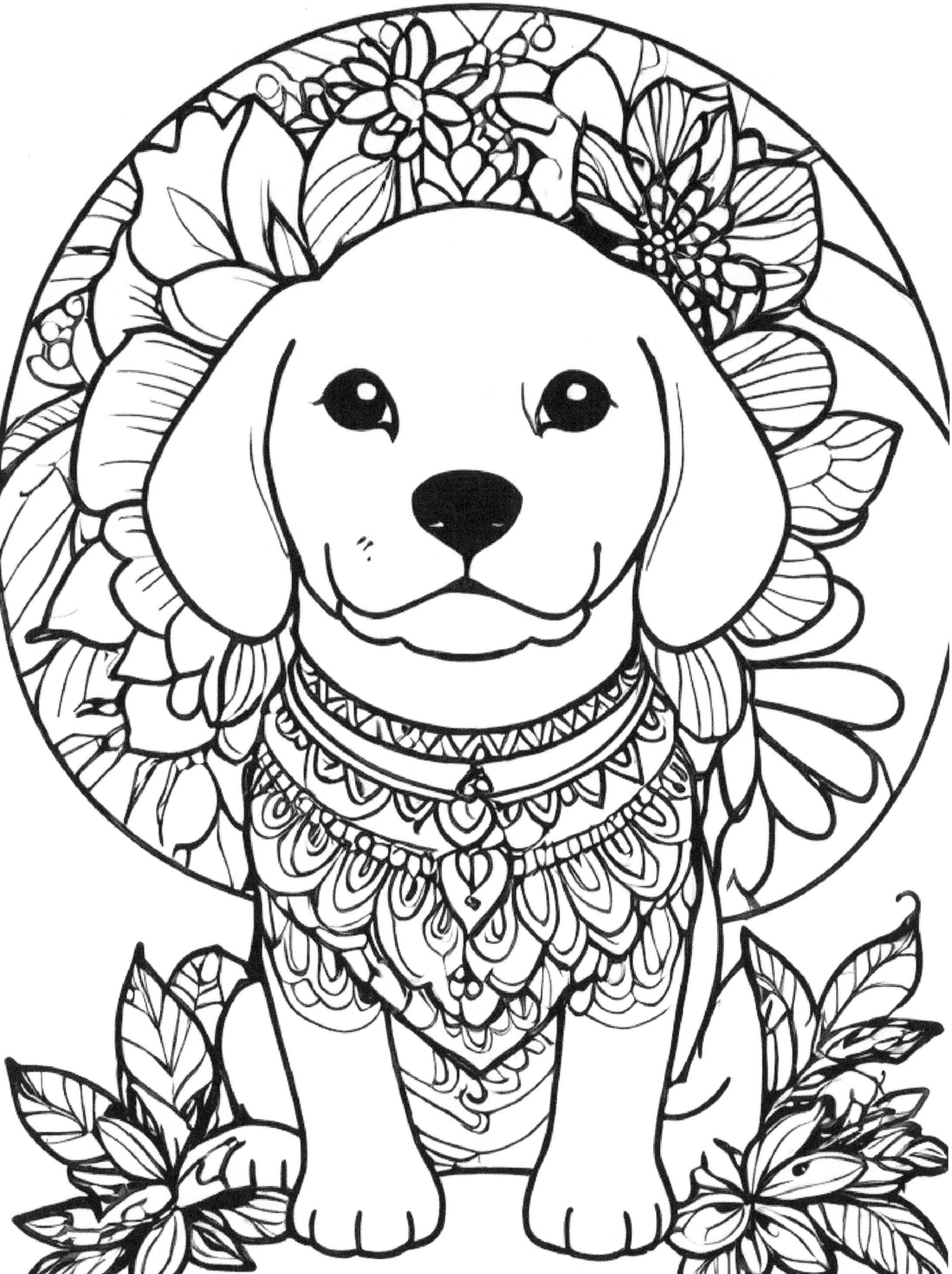

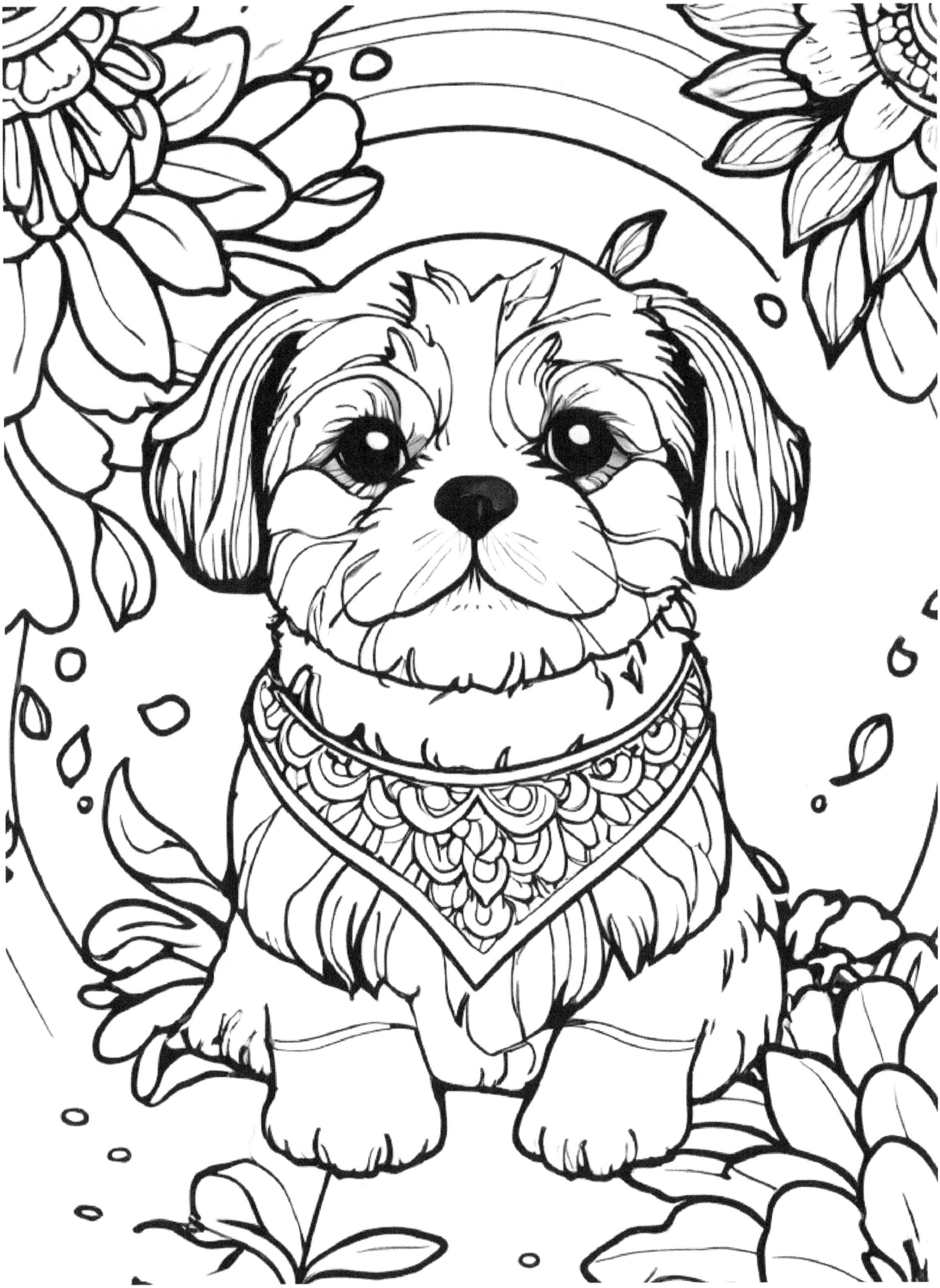

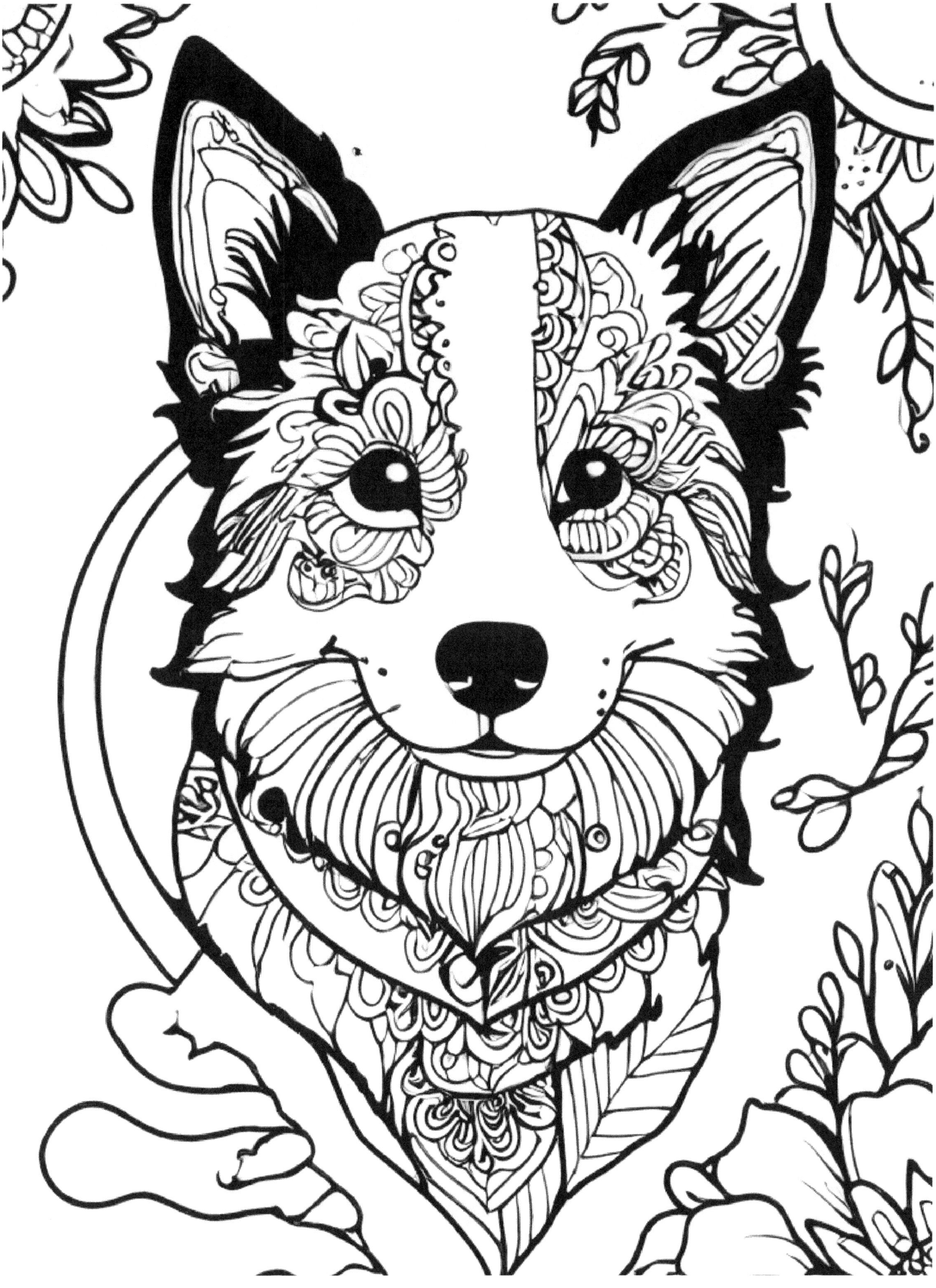

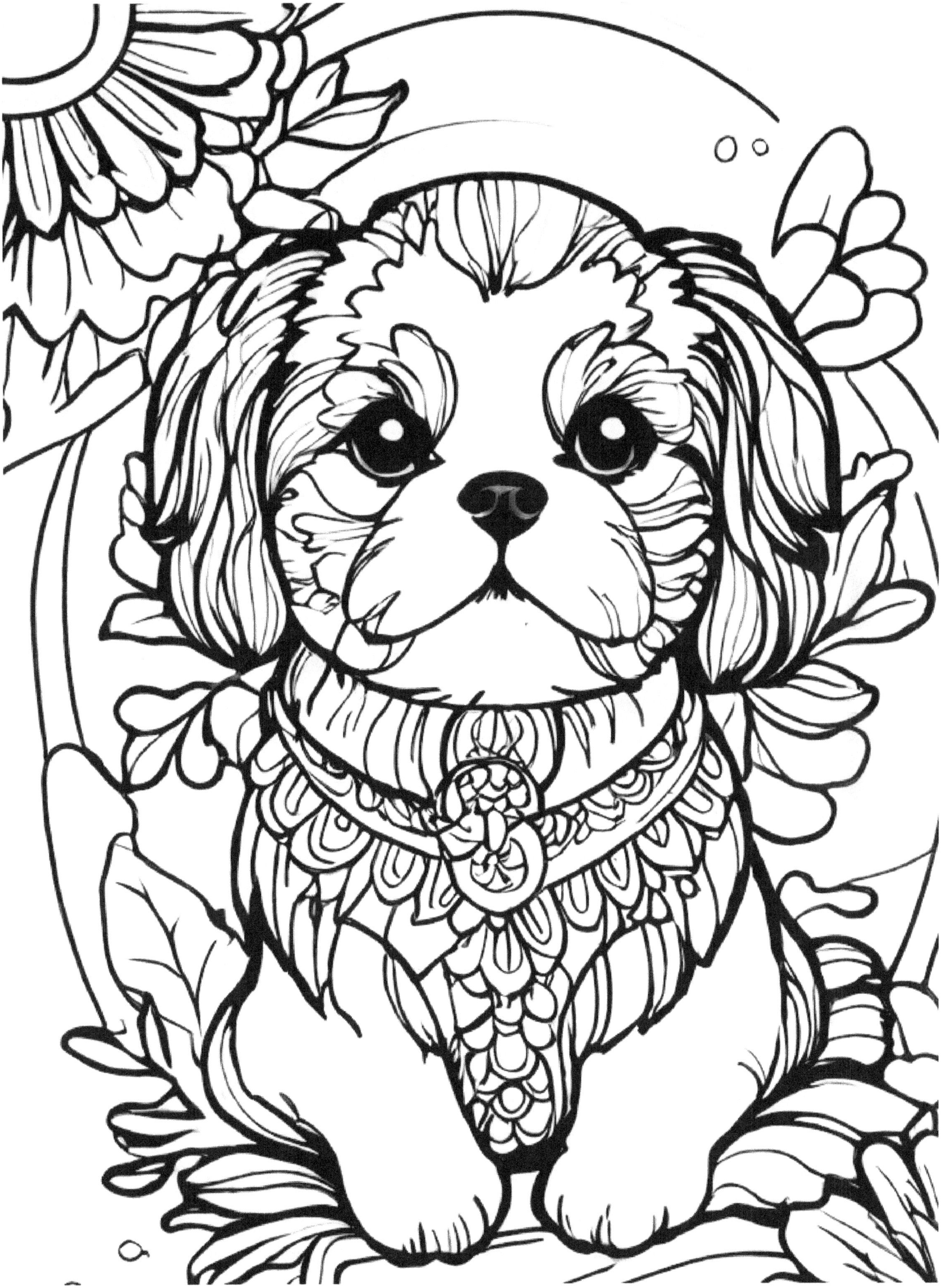

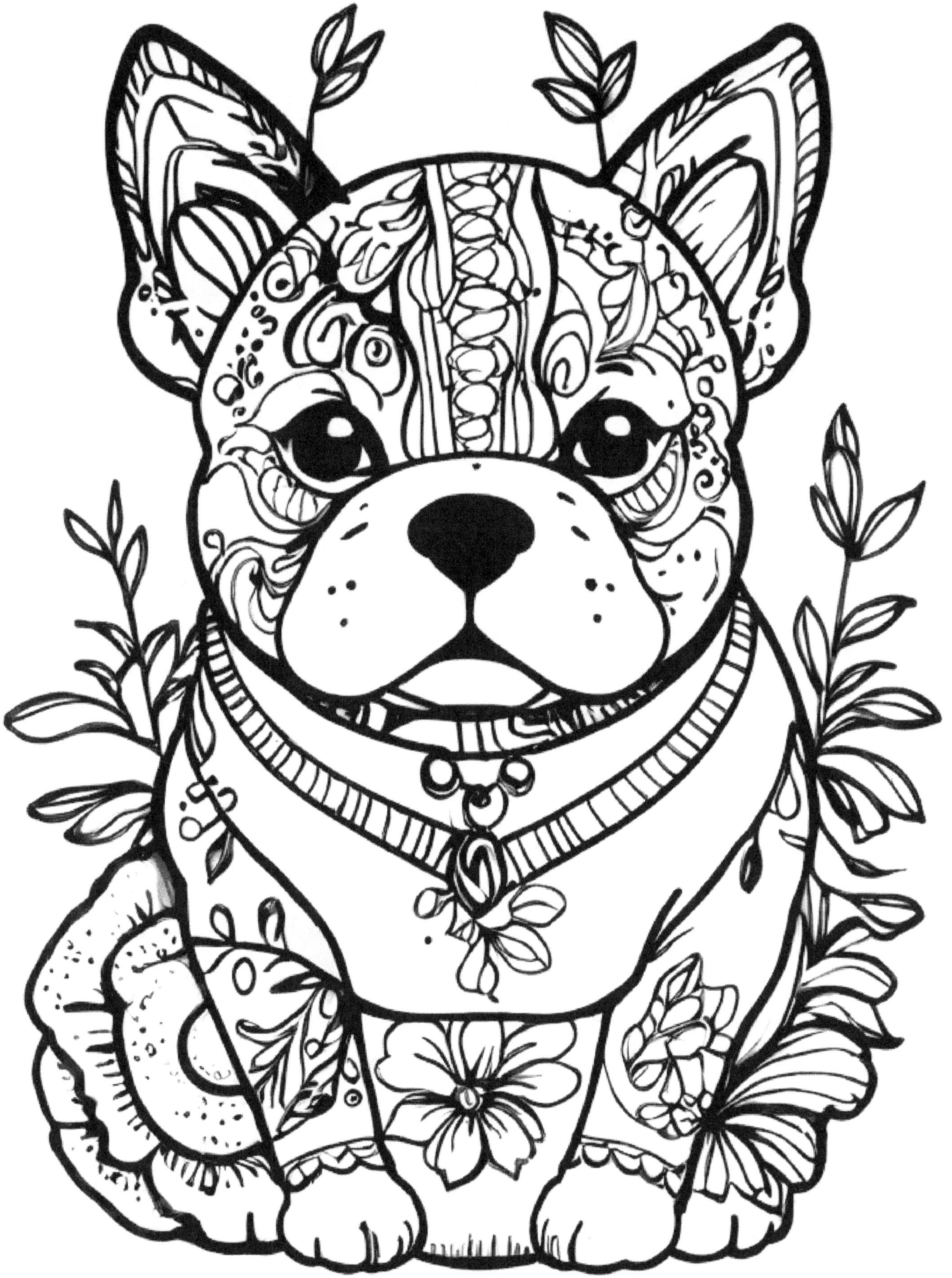

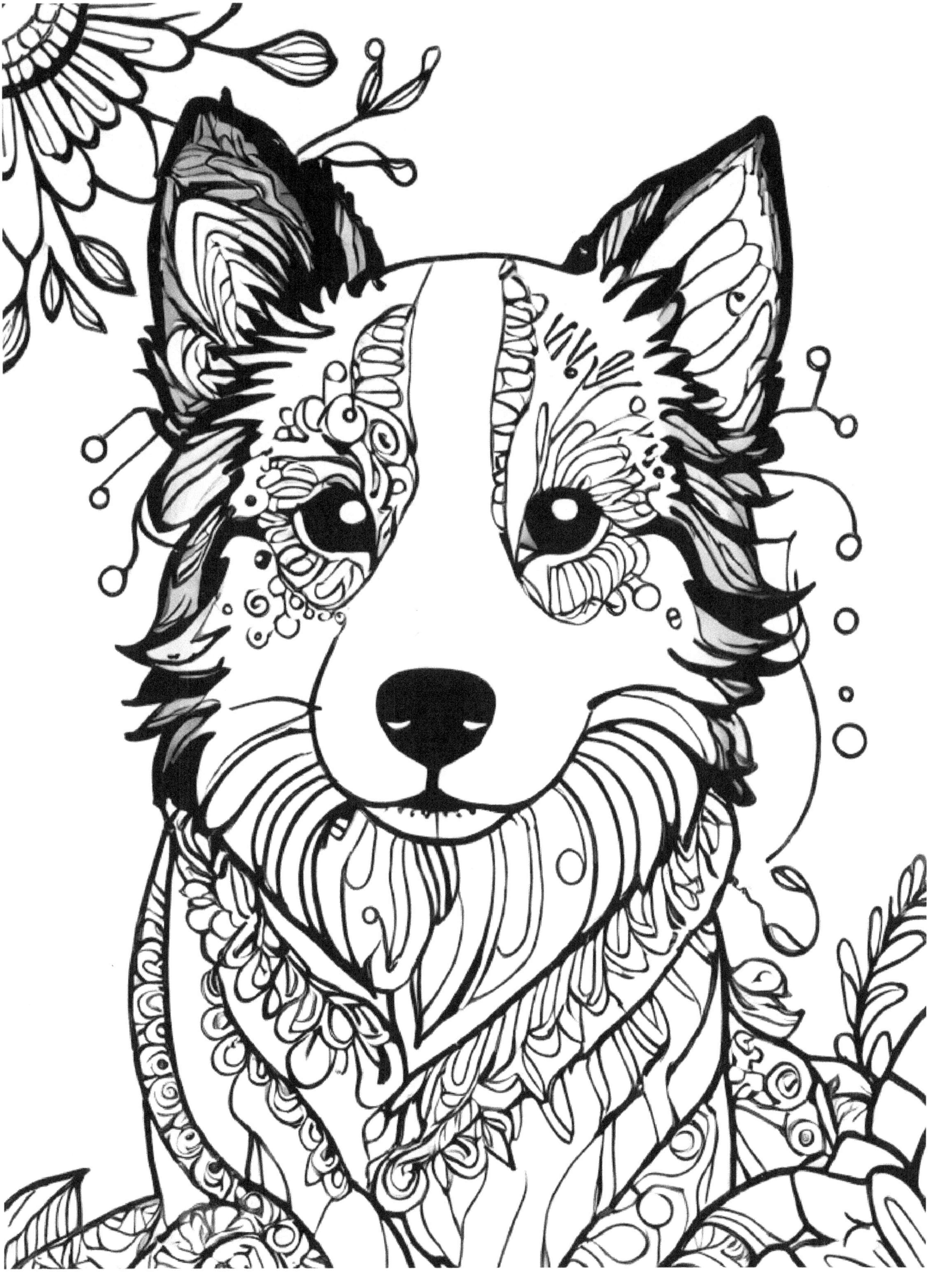

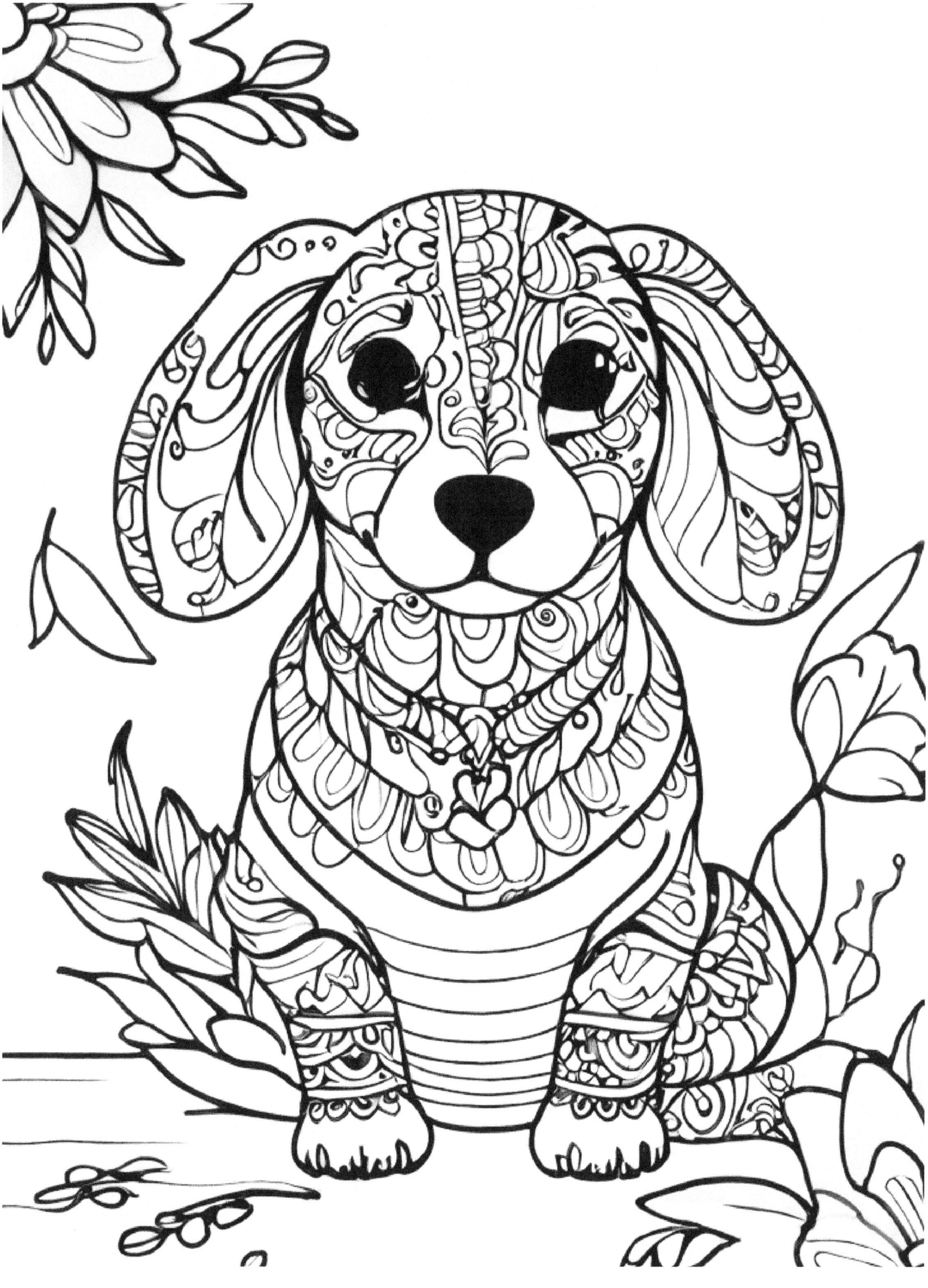

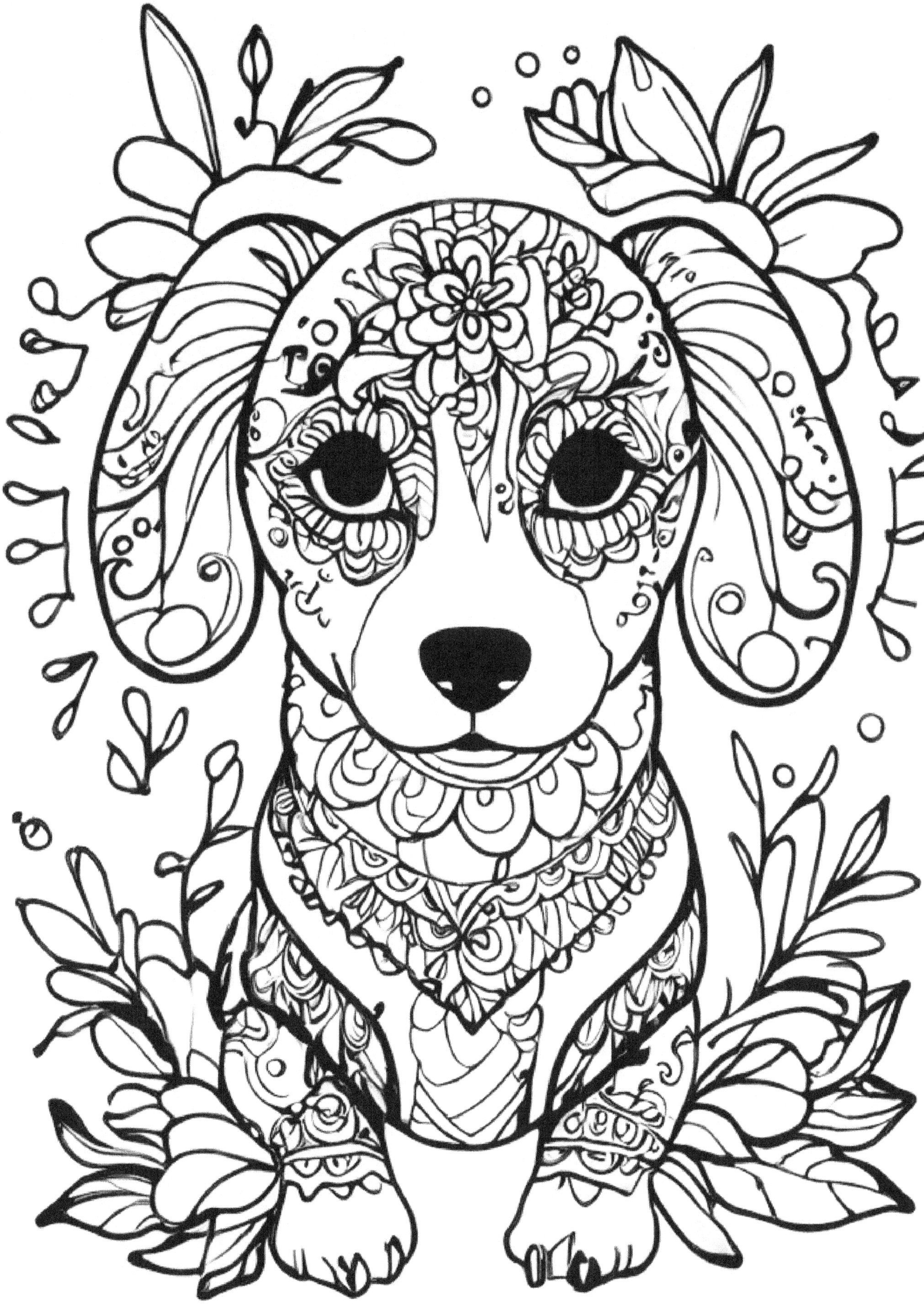

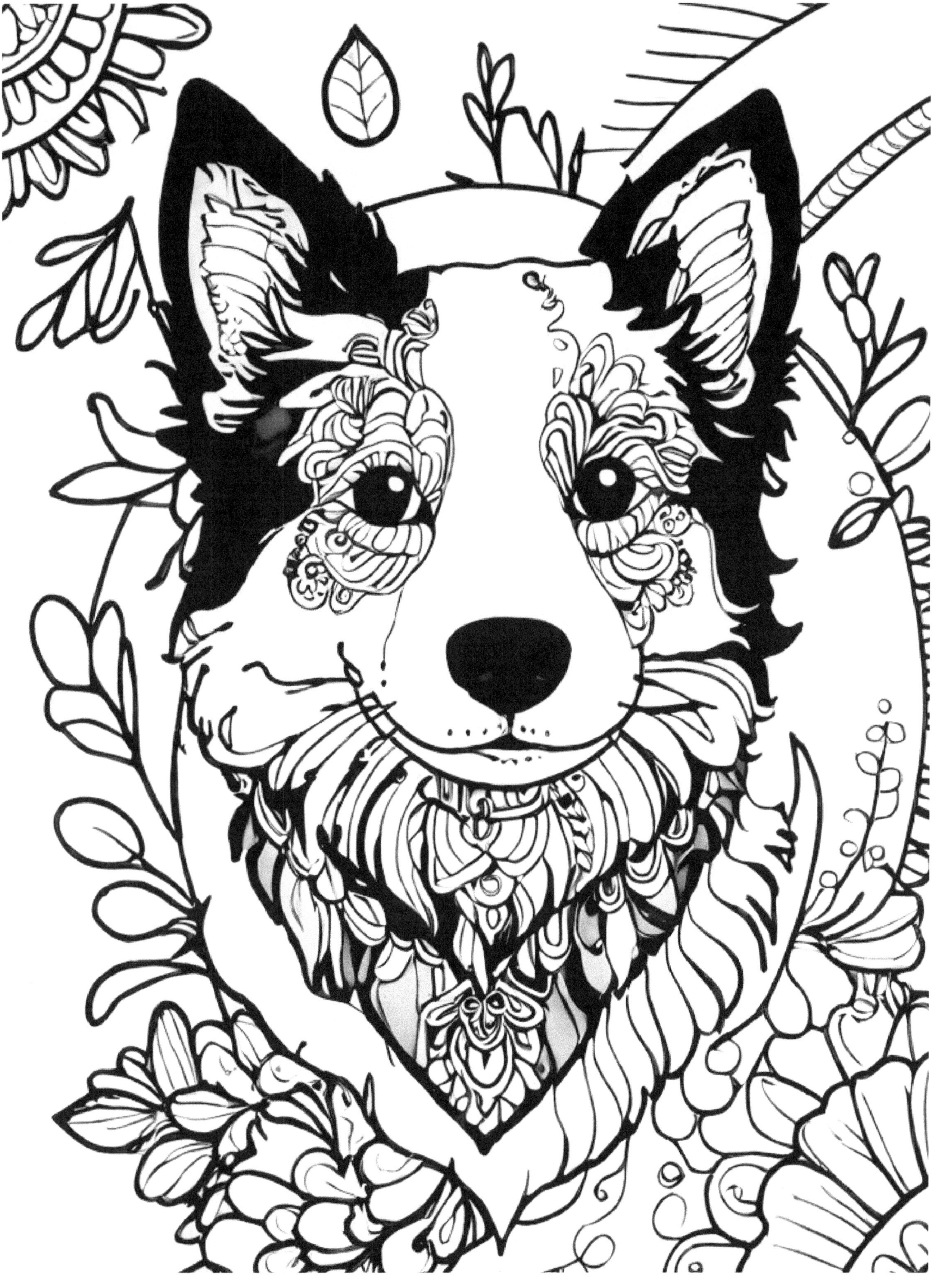

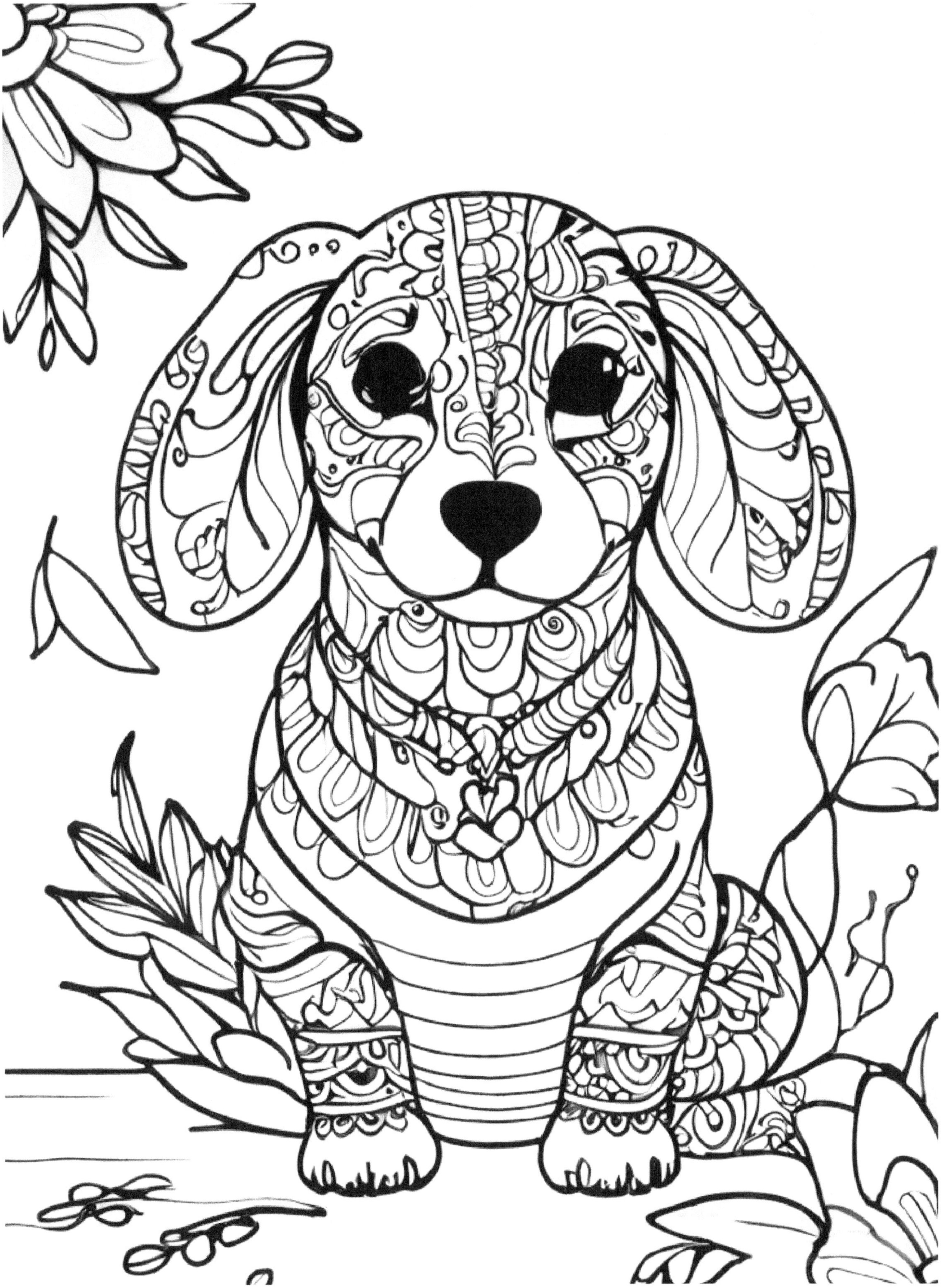

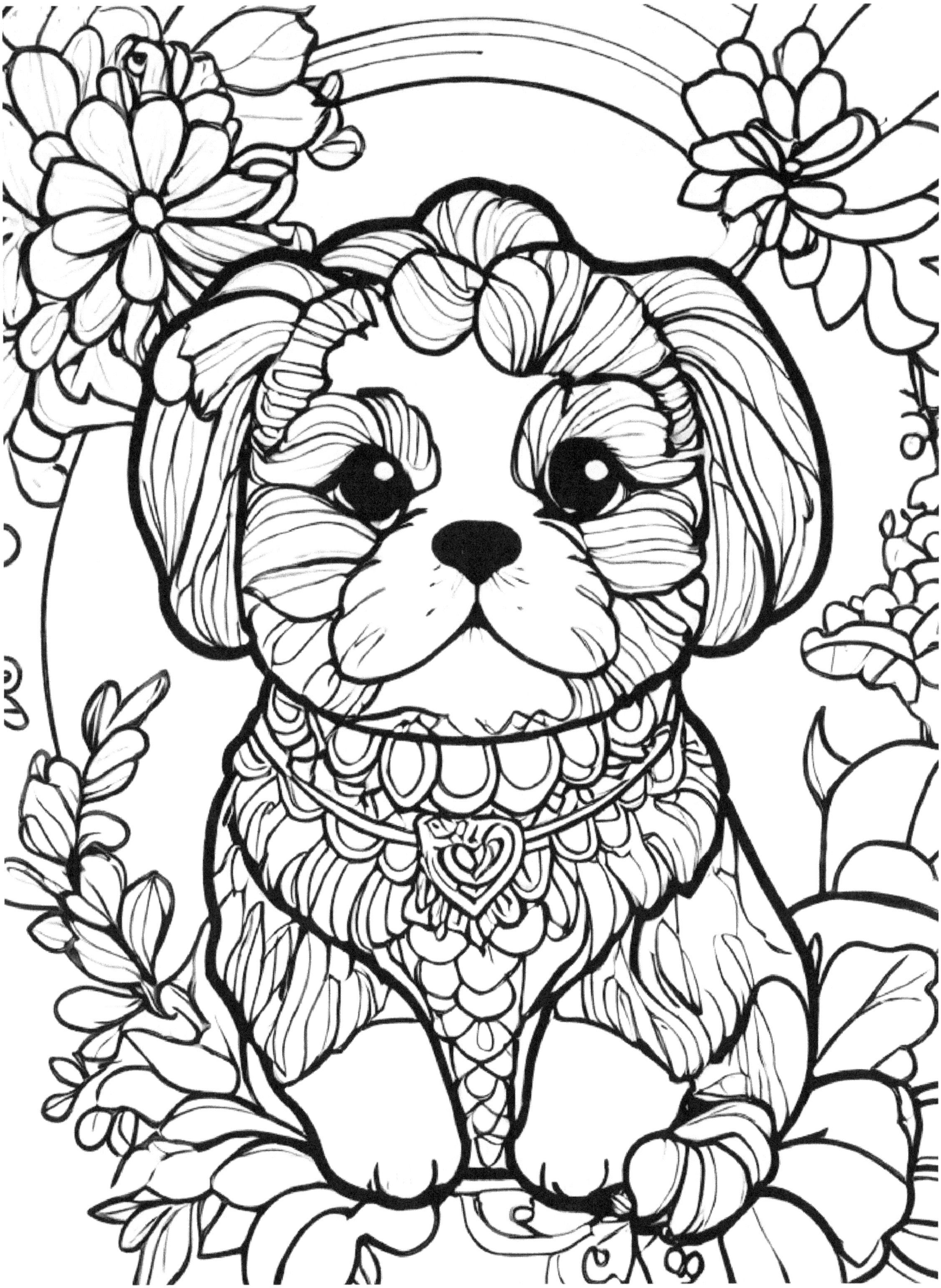

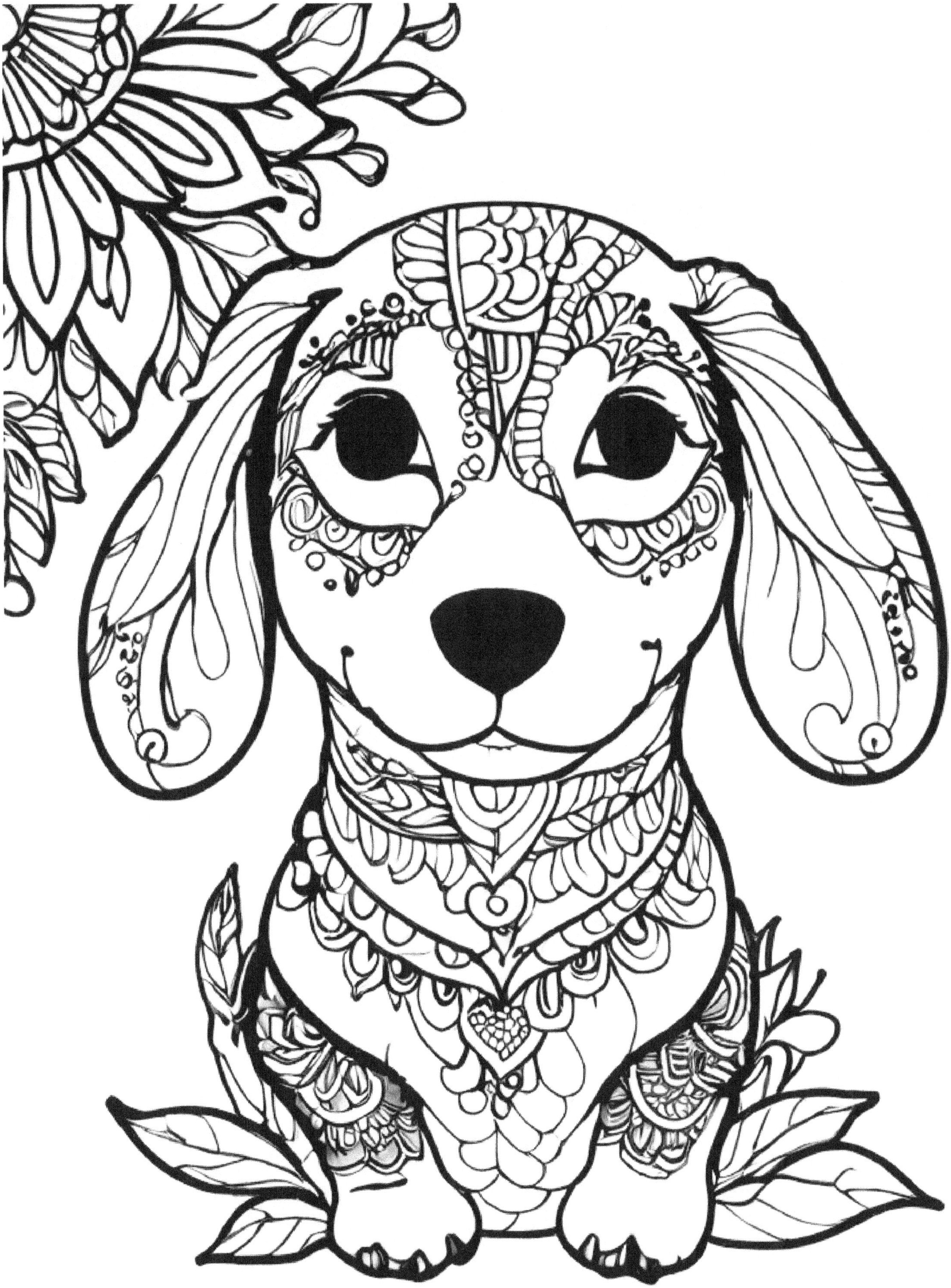

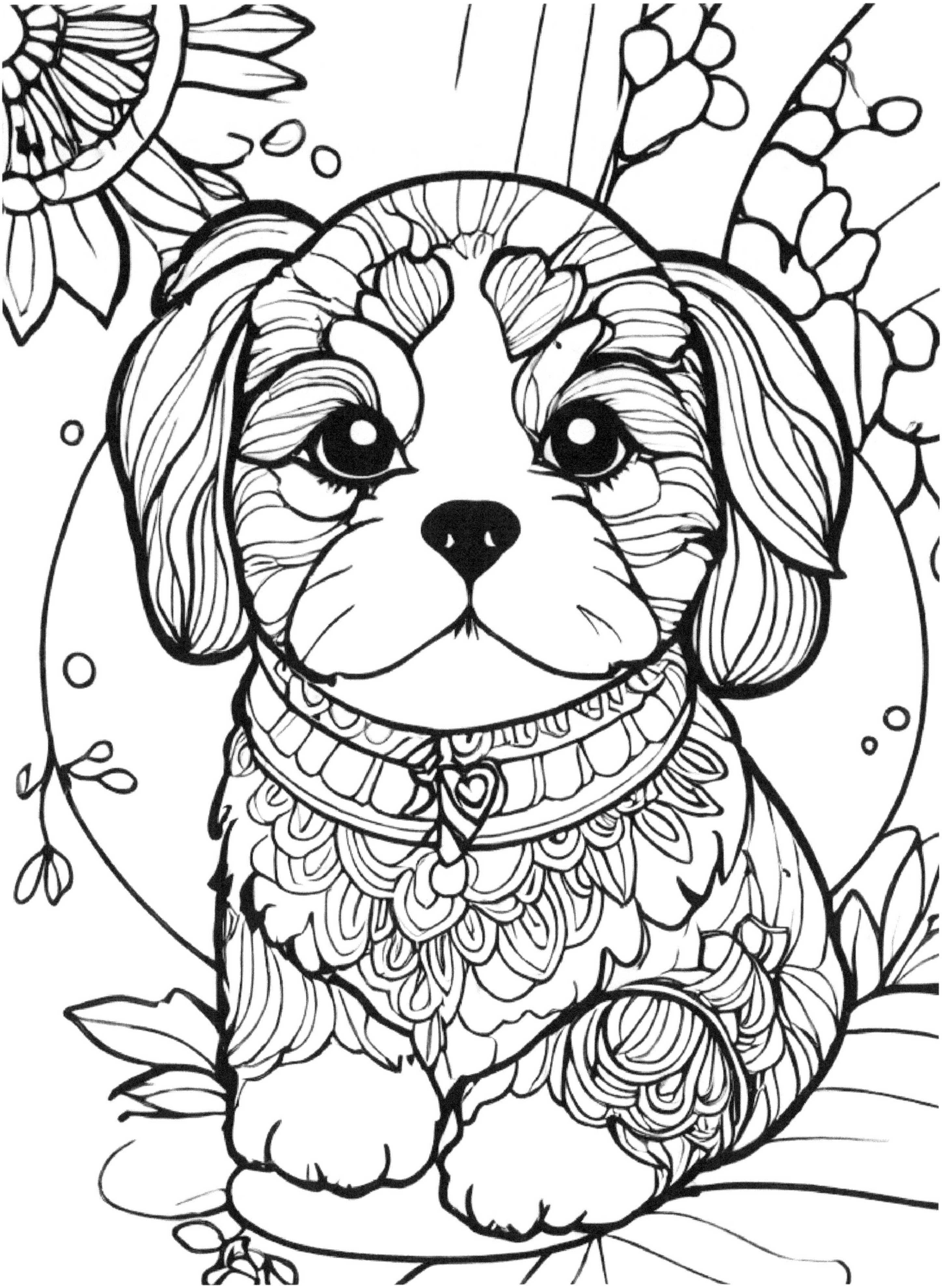

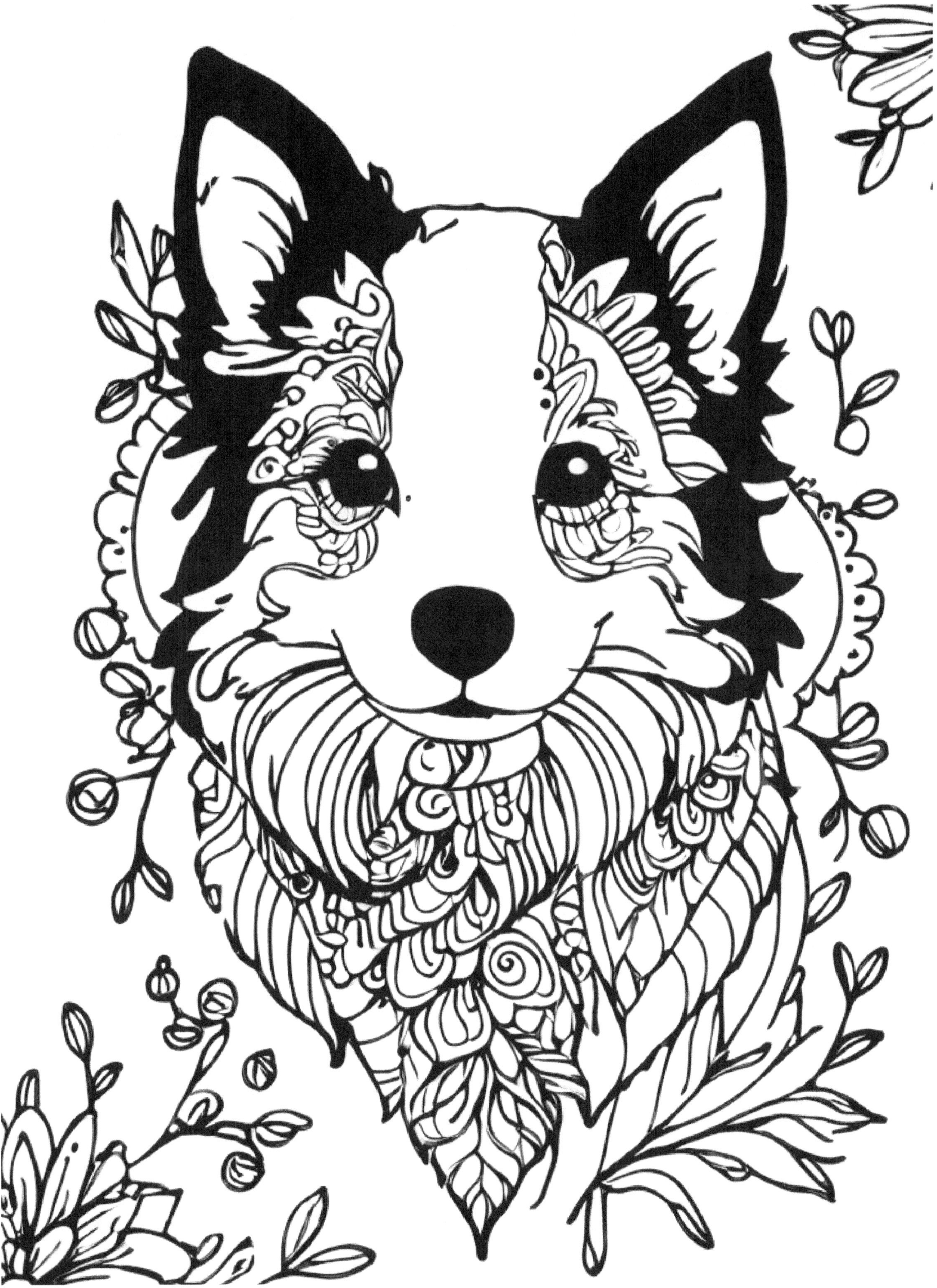

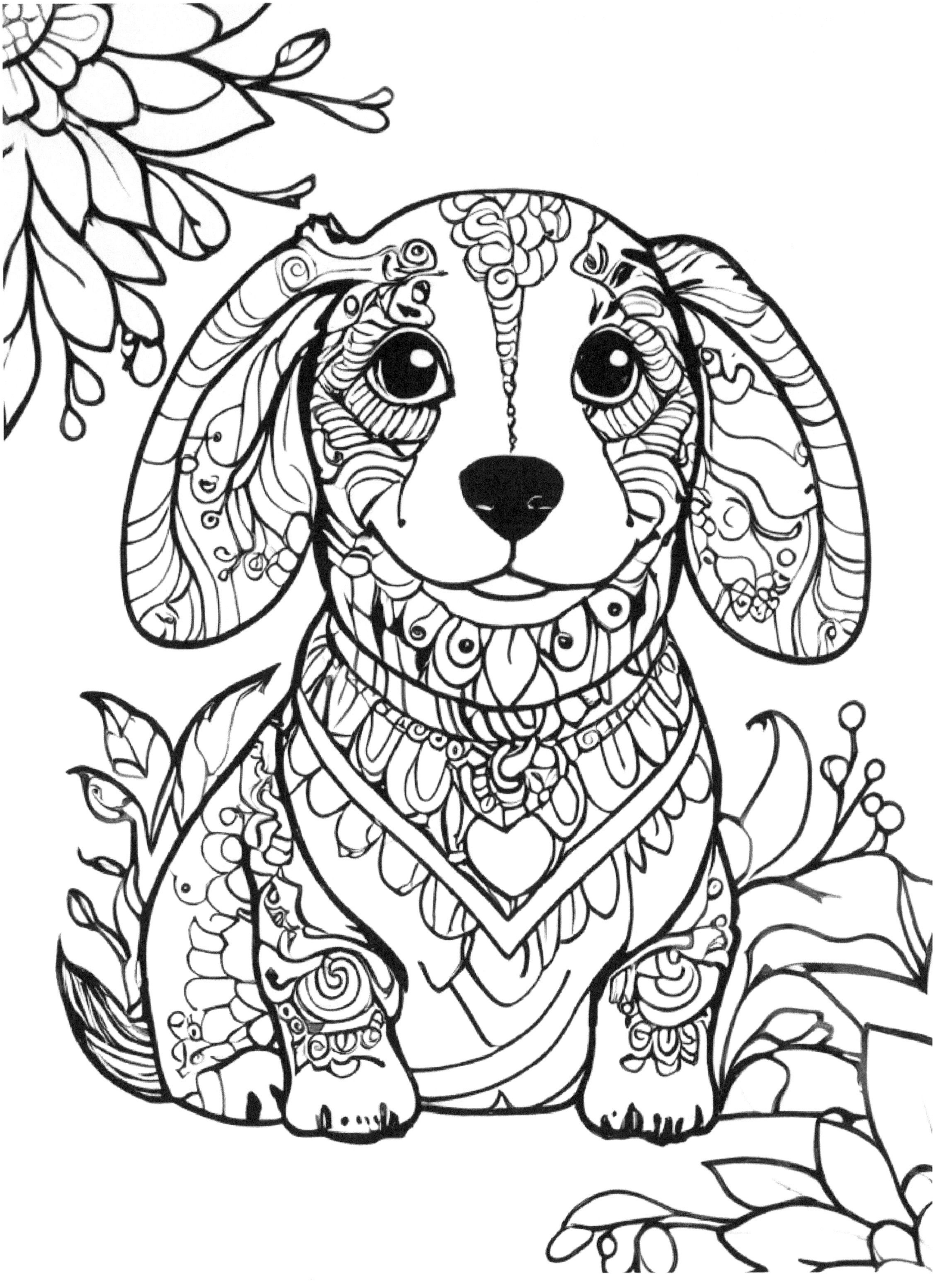

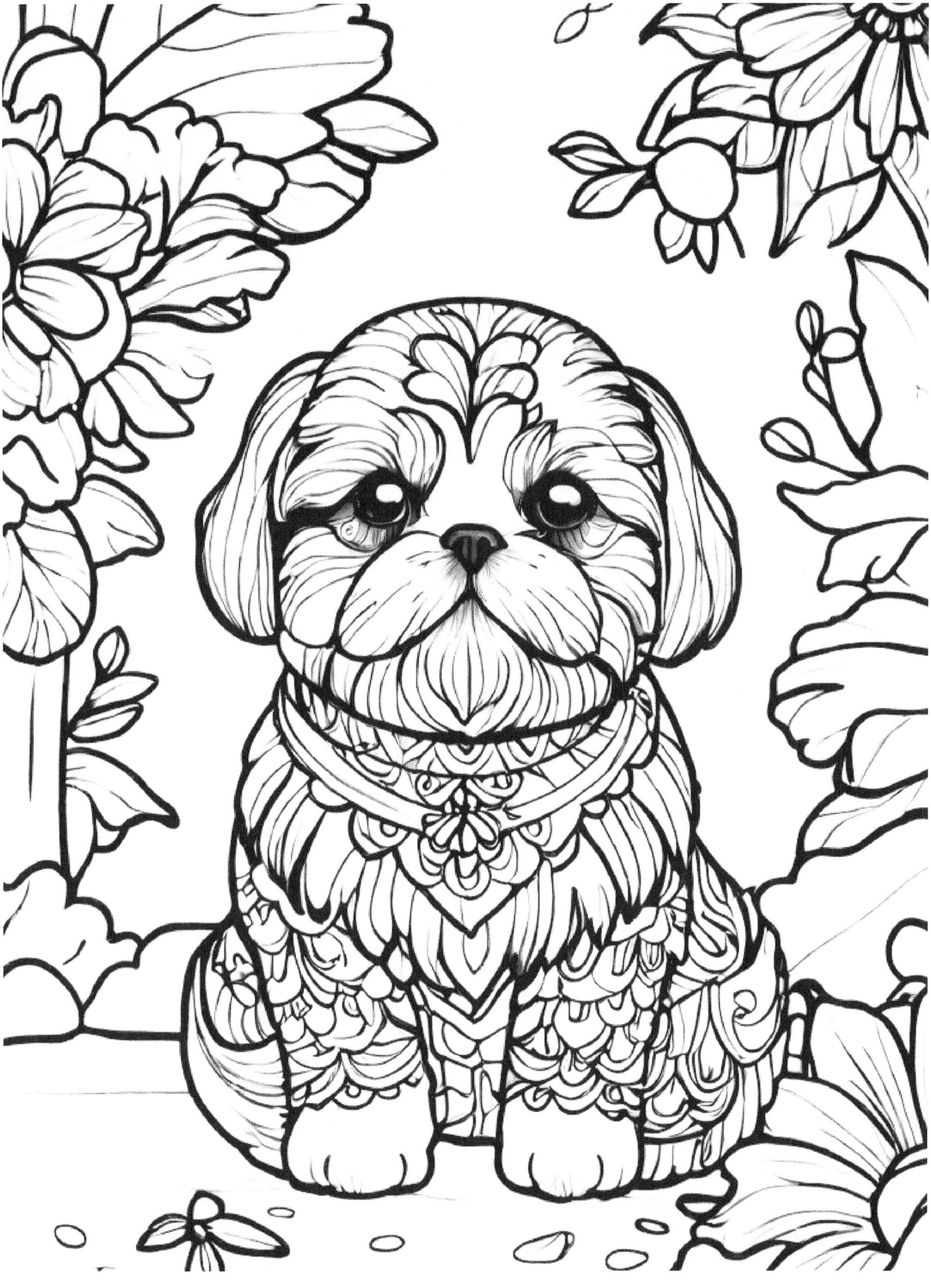

www.ingramcontent.com/pod-product-compliance
Lightning Source LLC
Chambersburg PA
CBHW081143290526
45795CB00006B/2359
9798880059393